Boland
1974

ETHIOPIA

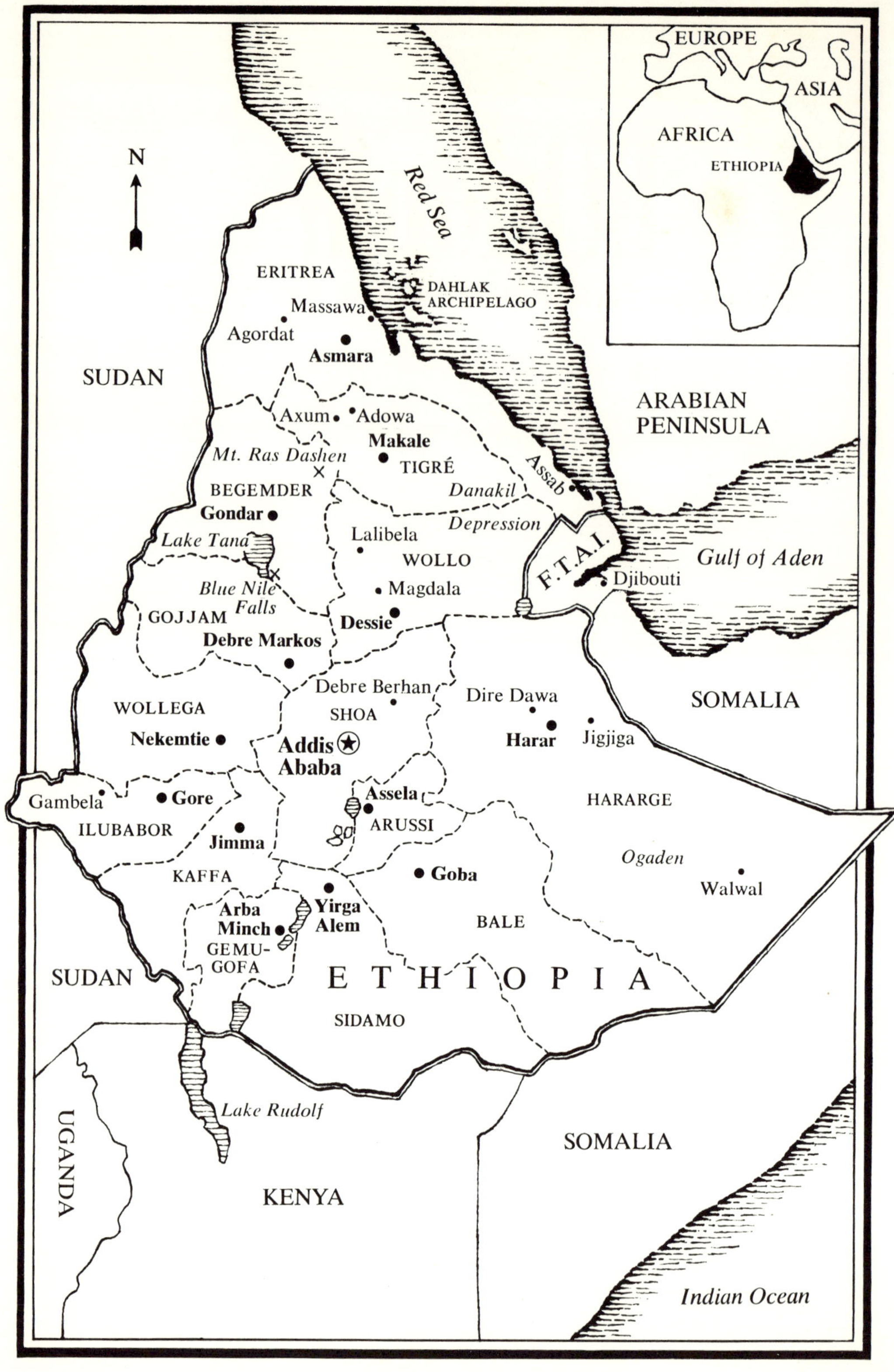
EUROPE
ASIA
AFRICA
ETHIOPIA
N
Red Sea
ERITREA
DAHLAK ARCHIPELAGO
Massawa
Agordat
Asmara
SUDAN
ARABIAN PENINSULA
Axum
Adowa
Makale
Mt. Ras Dashen
TIGRÉ
Assab
BEGEMDER
Danakil
Gondar
Depression
Lake Tana
Lalibela
WOLLO
Gulf of Aden
F.T.A.I.
Djibouti
Blue Nile Falls
Magdala
GOJJAM
Dessie
Debre Markos
Debre Berhan
Dire Dawa
SOMALIA
WOLLEGA
SHOA
Harar
Jigjiga
Nekemtie
Addis Ababa
Gambela
Gore
Assela
HARARGE
ILUBABOR
ARUSSI
Jimma
Ogaden
KAFFA
Goba
Walwal
Arba Minch
Yirga Alem
BALE
GEMU-GOFA
SUDAN
ETHIOPIA
SIDAMO
Lake Rudolf
UGANDA
SOMALIA
KENYA
Indian Ocean

Ethiopia

LAND OF THE LION

BY LILA PERL

illustrated with 67 photographs

William Morrow and Company
New York 1972

Printed in the United States of America.
1 2 3 4 5 76 75 74 73 72

Perl, Lila.
Ethiopia, land of the lion.

SUMMARY: Discusses the geography, history, religions, education, economy, and culture of Africa's oldest independent monarchy.
1. Ethiopia—Juvenile literature. [1. Ethiopia]
I. Title.
DT373.P35 916.3'03'6 72-1543
ISBN 0-688-20033-8
ISBN 0-688-30033-2 (lib. bdg.)

ACKNOWLEDGMENTS

The author wishes to express her gratitude to the following for their generous assistance and valued cooperation:

His Excellency Ato Habte Selassie Tafesse, Administrator, Ethiopian Tourist Organization; Ato Gebre Michael Kidane, Deputy Administrator, Ethiopian Tourist Organization; Mr. J. L. Brumit, General Manager, Ethiopian Airlines; Ato Yohannes Kifle, Director, Sales Promotion and Public Relations, Ethiopian Airlines; Mr. David J. DuBois, Director, United States Information Service, Addis Ababa; Mr. Edward W. M. Bryant, Commercial Attaché, United States Embassy, Addis Ababa; Mr. Walter Menke, Trans World Airlines; Woizero Elizabeth Yemane Berhan, Public Relations Director, Ethiopian Tourist Organization; Ato Kifle Seyoum, Administrator, Ethiopian Tourist Organization Branch Office, Gondar; Ato Gebre Hiwot, Administrator, Ethiopian Tourist Organization Branch Office, Asmara; Captain Atnafu Makonnen, Administrator, Haile Selassie I Theater, Addis Ababa; Woizero Manna M. Mengesha, Principal, W. Zerfeshiwal School, Addis Ababa; Mr. Reinhold Aignherr, General Manager, Addis Ababa Hilton Hotel; Mr. B. T. Bowyer, United Touring Company, Addis Ababa.

All photographs are by Lila Perl with the exception of the following from the Ethiopian Tourist Organization: pp. 12, 15, 19, 21, 22, 25, 30, 32, 34, 53, 57, 63, 65, 66, 80, 93, 96, 97, 106, 108, 124, 126, 127, 128, 130, 145, 149, 150. Permission is gratefully acknowledged.

CONTENTS

I

LAND OF THE LION

FOR OVER TWO THOUSAND YEARS, ETHIOPIA HAS SAT IN proud and splendid isolation atop some of the highest mountain terrain in Africa. Unlike every other country on the African continent, the Empire of Ethiopia never experienced full-scale colonization by a foreign power and is today the oldest independent monarchy in Africa.

Throughout history, while Romans, Vandals, Byzantines, and Arabs took turns dominating northern Africa, while the nations of Europe carved out colonial possessions both north and south of the Sahara, Ethiopia remained astonishingly free of foreign control. Its people kept to their own customs, traditions, and religion, developed their own agricultural patterns, school systems, and art forms, and were ruled by their own countrymen.

By the beginning of the twentieth century, Africa was a mass of captive peoples. On the entire continent there were only two independent countries: Liberia, in West Africa, which had been established as a Negro republic in 1847, and the ancient Empire of Ethiopia, located inside the wedge-shaped "horn" of Africa's east coast.

Ethiopia has been called "the land of the lion," because the king of beasts has always been the symbol of strength, pride, and individual leadership in that country. It is traditional for the Ethiopian warrior who has killed a lion to go into battle wearing a lion-mane headdress or a cape of lion skin. Even in the Italo-Ethiopian War of 1935-36, the local chieftains encouraged their soldiers to wear their lion skins against the machine guns, heavy artillery, and mustard gas of Mussolini's well-equipped armies. Ethiopian monarchs have almost always kept a pet lion cub or two close to their persons, and cages of lions have usually been a feature of their palace compounds.

How did it happen that Ethiopia managed to maintain its independence, except for the brief Italian occupation, while most of its African neighbors did not even begin to emerge from their years of foreign control until the 1960's?

The reason for its traditional independence lies chiefly in the forbidding terrain of the Ethiopian highlands. Even today Ethiopia's craggy heartland as well as its low-lying desert and jungle fringe lands have not been fully explored or charted. In fact, it is only in the years since World War II that the outside world has begun to know very much about the hidden and mysterious land of Ethiopia.

The land of the lion is enormous. It covers 470,000 square miles, an area a little larger than the combined territory of Texas, Oklahoma, and New Mexico. It is bordered on the northeast by the Red Sea and on the southeast by Somalia. Ethiopia's neighbor to the south is Kenya. The Sudan lies to the west and northwest.

The Ethiopians divide their country into regions in terms of elevation. There are three distinct climate zones: the *kwolla,* the *woina dega,* and the *dega.*

The *kwolla* is the hot zone. It applies to the low-lying areas of Ethiopia that are found near the present-day borders of the Empire. As Ethiopia lies only a couple of hundred miles north of the equator, between the equator and the Tropic of Cancer, the *kwolla* deserts and jungles and the steamy port towns of the Red Sea coast all have typically tropical climates. *Kwolla* regions with adequate rainfall grow cotton, sugarcane, coffee, oil seeds, and tropical fruits.

Tropical weather is not the case, however, throughout most of the country. Within the fringe of lowlands, there rises a high plateau and mountain region with temperate to cool temperatures.

At elevations of from 5000 to 8000 feet, the Ethiopian high country is known as the *woina dega* (highland of the grape). The farmers who live here grow grains such as wheat, barley, millet, and sorghum, as well as legumes such as lentils, chick peas, and beans. Grapevines, olive trees, and many kinds of fruits and vegetables can also be grown in this zone.

Addis Ababa, the capital of Ethiopia, lies in the *woina dega* at an altitude of just under 8000 feet. Although the city is at a latitude of only nine degrees north of the equator, the temperature hovers between sixty and eighty degrees Fahrenheit throughout the year. The weather is sunny and pleasant except for the three-month rainy season, from June to September, which is known as the Ethiopian-highland "winter." At that time of year the weather becomes even cooler and Addis Ababans use electric or fuel-burning space heaters in order to keep comfortably warm when indoors.

At an elevation of 8000 feet or above, the land is known as the *dega* zone. These cooler highlands are best suited to cattle-raising, sheepherding, and to growing the hardier cereal grains such as barley.

Many highland peaks jut to 12,000 feet. Ethiopia's highest peak, Mount Ras Dashen in the Semien Mountains, rises to 15,158 feet and is the fourth highest mountain in Africa. Snow has been known to fall in the higher Semiens, even though Ethiopia is in the tropics.

An outstanding geographical feature of Ethiopia's central highlands is the Rift Valley, which cuts a diagonal swathe through the mountains. Running from northeast to southwest, the Rift creates dramatic cliffs with steep drops into the clefts and valleys thousands of feet below. All through the highlands the terrain is rugged and often treacherous.

Nevertheless, the highlands have been the preferred dwelling place of the Ethiopian people throughout history. Here

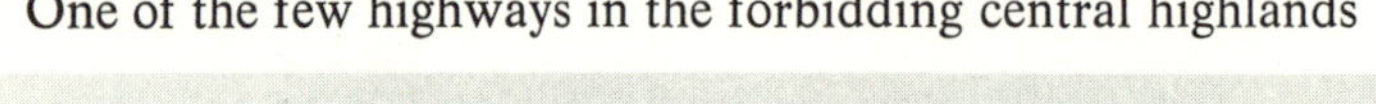

One of the few highways in the forbidding central highlands

they have been safe from the dreaded malarial mosquito and the tsetse fly. And here, too, they have found safety from foreign invaders and enemies within.

Most Ethiopians of the central highland provinces are a people known as the Amharas; those of the northern highland provinces are the Tigreans. The Amharas and Tigreans make up about one-third of the country's very varied population of 25 million. Although they are not the most numerous, they dominate Ethiopian society in religion, politics, economics, and social position.

Most Amharas and Tigreans are a mixture of the original Hamitic inhabitants of northern and eastern Africa and of the Semitic peoples who, beginning about 1000 B.C., came to the horn of Africa from southern Arabia across the Red Sea.

Amharas and Tigreans are usually dark-skinned with black, tightly curling hair. They often have the thin lips, straight narrow noses, high foreheads, and large luminous eyes of their Hamitic forebears. Others show a strong Semitic strain—the slightly down-curving noses and fuller lips of the Arabian peoples who intermarried with them. Despite their generally dark skins, Amharas and Tigreans are classified racially as Caucasians.

Their languages, Amharic and Tigrinya, are Semitic tongues and are related to Hebrew and Arabic, but are written in their own unique lettering. Although tens of languages and hundreds of dialects are spoken in Ethiopia, Amharic is the official tongue.

The Amharas and the Tigreans are Christians, members of the Ethiopian Monophysite Church, which is the state church of the Empire. In fact, Ethiopia is one of the oldest

The *tukul* of the Amhara highlander

Christian countries in the world and the only African country in which Christianity has been the official religion since the fourth century.

The typical Amhara of the central highlands lives today just as his ancestors did in early Christian times—in a round hut with mud-plaster walls and a cone-shaped roof of thatch, called a *tukul*. He scrapes his existence from the soil, growing millet for the flour for his daily pancake-bread, wheat and barley, peas and beans. Land-irrigation systems are few, and crop-planting is geared to the single annual rainy season. Most peasants also have herds of sheep, goats, and cattle.

There are not many cities, towns, or even villages, and roads are almost nonexistent in mountainous Ethiopia. The wheel, which was so important to the progress of man, has been of very limited use here. Native wheeled vehicles are

A group of Amhara homesteads atop an *amba*

seldom seen on the stony dirt paths that thread their way through the Ethiopian highlands. Most journeys are made on foot; the more prosperous Amhara travels by mule. The most efficient method of transportation is by air.

Amhara country people are as proud and independent as their land of the lion. They do not tend to live clustered together in villages. The Amhara peasant likes to build his homestead of one or more *tukuls* on the top of an *amba,* a flat-topped hill.

Ambas are very common in the Ethiopian high country. Once upon a time, these strange-looking rises must have been cone-shaped. Due to erosion, their tops have become flattened and the soil carried down their sides, so that there is often greenery growing around the base of the *amba* even in the dry season. There are no visible roads or paths up its

An Amhara woman dressed in *shamma* and *k'amis* at a village market

steep sides. Yet the Ethiopian farmer does descend it to work in his fields, to graze his animals, to make the weekly trip to market, to visit the district church. The typical Amhara homestead or settlement is encircled by a stone wall. Among the *tukuls* sit the precious mounds of dull-yellow grain harvested at the end of the last growing season.

The most important article of clothing among Amharas and Tigreans is the *shamma*—a three-yard-long rectangular shawl tossed togalike over the shoulder and upper half of the body. White cotton jodhpurs, or white trousers, and sandals, complete the costume for the man. Women wear the *shamma* over a *k'amis,* a white cotton dress with a full swinging skirt, which may come to the mid-calf or to the knee. For more festive occasions, the *shamma* and the skirt of the dress are bordered with colorful embroidery.

A Galla child of eastern Ethiopia

Even the Ethiopian city man, dressed in shirt, tie, and dark business suit, will often drape the *shamma* over his other apparel. And the trim young secretaries who work in Addis Ababa's modern offices occasionally wear native dress to their jobs. Many like to wear the *shamma* and *k'amis* when they go out on a date, to a restaurant, a film, or a discotheque. Both men and women sometimes wear the *shamma* as a head-covering as well.

By far the most numerous of Ethiopia's population groups are a people called the Galla, who are estimated to make up nearly half the country's population. Like the Amharas and the Tigreans, the Galla are a Hamitic people. They, too, have intermarried with Semitic peoples from southern Arabia, and they are also related to the Somali, who live on Ethiopia's eastern and southern borders. Until the sixteenth century, the Galla lived mainly in southern Ethiopia. Then, pushed northward by the Somalis, the Galla migrated into Christian territory. Today they are widely scattered throughout the Empire. They are divided into about two hundred tribal groups and are quite varied in their religion, customs, and life style, depending largely on where they have settled.

Most Galla are Moslems, although some have adopted Christianity and some follow animistic religions. Dark-skinned and usually with rather broader features than the Amharas and Tigreans, the Galla are also a Caucasian people. Their basic language is Galla, which belongs to the Cushitic language family.

A large group of Galla people live in Hararge Province, in eastern Ethiopia, in the vicinity of the intermediate-highland towns of Dire Dawa and Harar. These Galla are Moslems and also speak Arabic, which is common throughout eastern Ethiopia. Many Galla dwell in the arid foothill country outside Dire Dawa and live in huts that are partially dug into the sides of the knolls that dot the landscape. The walls and roofs of the huts are plastered with dry caked mud. The Galla of this region keep camels, which supply milk and meat and also serve as beasts of burden.

At a slightly higher elevation, not far from the old walled city of Harar, the Galla along with the Somali, Arab, and other folk of the vicinity, gather *chat,* or *khat,* which they sell at the local markets. This green, leafy plant grows wild on the hillsides. The leaves, when chewed, act as a stimulant and are said to produce a pleasant "high." Taken in excess, *chat* can bring on a narcotic stupor.

Chat is used extensively by the Moslems of eastern Ethiopia and is an important item of export to the Yemen and other parts of the Arabian peninsula, where it does not grow without cultivation. It is much in demand by Moslem peoples, as their religion forbids the use of alcoholic stimulants.

The Galla of eastern Ethiopia are strikingly different in their manner of dress from their white-clad Amhara and Tigrean countrymen of the central and northern highlands. The Galla women are particularly colorful. Bare-shouldered, upper arms flashing with silver bracelets, they dress in artfully draped and knotted garments, always accented with flashes of color. Rich warm saffrons and glowing reds are their favorites.

While the Amhara mother carries her baby on her back, often completely concealed in a fine white cotton shawl to ward off dirt, disease, and the evil eye, the Galla mother is just as likely to sling her baby across her hip along with other small bundles. At the same time she balances on her head a laden tray, a basket, a large pottery jug, or even a bundle

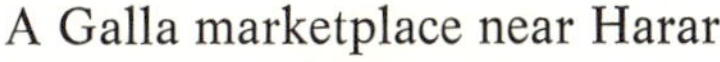

A Galla marketplace near Harar

of firewood. Her arms swing free and her walk is proud and graceful. Her hair is usually worn drawn back into two buns that rest behind her ears.

The eastern lowlands are *kwolla* regions of intense tropical heat. On the 670-mile Red Sea coast in northeastern Ethiopia, the coastal strip is narrow, sandy, and desolate. Temperatures reach 120 degrees in the Red Sea port town of Massawa and the humidity is very high, although rainfall is scarce.

Sleepy, sweltering Massawa has a population of 20,000, which includes many Arab-Moslem peoples. In the 1500's Massawa was taken by the Turks and remained under Turkish control for three hundred years. Today Massawa lives off shipping and the extraction of salt from seawater, which has resulted in a local salt industry with a considerable export trade.

The only other places of any importance on Ethiopia's Red Sea coast are the port of Assab, which lies at the extreme southeastern tip of the Red Sea, and the ruins of the old city of Adulis, about thirty-five miles south of Massawa. Adulis was an active trading center in ancient times.

East of Massawa, about thirty-five miles off the coast, lie Ethiopia's Red Sea islands known as the Dahlak Archipelago. The Dahlaks consist of two larger islands and one hundred and twenty-four smaller islands, most of them uninhabited. Flat, arid, extremely hot, and almost completely undeveloped, the islands have a population of about 2500, mostly Arabs. One of their few occupations is pearl fishing. Like Massawa, the Dahlaks belonged to Turkey from the mid-sixteenth to the mid-nineteenth century.

Inland from the Red Sea coast lies one of Ethiopia's two largest arid-lowland areas, the inhospitable Danakil Depres-

Massawa, an old Arab-Moslem town
and a port on Ethiopia's Red Sea coast

sion, which is close to the border with Somalia and is inhabited by fierce, knife-bearing warrior-tribesmen, principally of Somali origin.

The blazing Danakil desert descends to nearly 400 feet below sea level. Its nomadic peoples with their camels, goats, and movable huts of matted grass or tents of animal skin live chiefly from animal herding and salt mining.

Rich pools of brine lie just beneath the Danakil's surface. Once the whitish, alkaline desert crust has been hacked away, the water content of the exposed brine evaporates rapidly in the hot sun. The salt then can be mined in blocks and loaded onto the backs of camels for transport to market. In some parts of the Danakil, salt blocks are still used in place of money.

Outsiders are not welcomed in the primitive and suspicious world of the Danakil tribesmen. The scarce water holes are jealously guarded, and strangers who go into the area armed are as vulnerable as those who go in unarmed, for the Danakil warriors are eager for rifles and other firearms and have been known to murder travelers on sight to obtain their weapons. The Danakils are Moslems and their allegiance is more often to their local sheiks than to the central Ethiopian government.

The nomadic peoples of the eastern lowlands keep camels, which they use as beasts of burden.

The largest lowland area in eastern Ethiopia is the Ogaden, a vast semidesert of stunted and thorny vegetation lying in the triangular southeastern corner of the country, near the border with Somalia. Here, too, the population is made up of nomadic herdsmen, with goats and camels the principal livestock, although some hardy grains are grown. Water holes are scarce and precious, however, and the rights to them are vigorously defended. The people of the Ogaden, who are mainly Somalis, have the reputation of being even fiercer than the Danakils.

Continuing clockwise around the fringes of Ethiopia, we come to the border with Kenya on the south. The borderland here is relatively high savanna country, subtropical in climate and rich in game. Farther to the west, Ethiopia's string of Rift Valley Lakes descends in a southwesterly direction almost to the point of meeting Kenya's Lake Rudolf.

Along the southwestern border with the Sudan, Ethiopia is at its most lushly tropical, with thick grasslands and patches of forest and jungle that teem with animal life. Kaffa Province is said to be the original home of the wild coffee plants that help to make up Ethiopia's major export crop.

The adjoining and lower-lying province of Ilubabor experiences the hot weather of the *kwolla* zone and has the wettest climate in Ethiopia. There is an average rainfall of eighty inches a year here, as compared with forty in Addis Ababa and twenty in Asmara, capital of Eritrea Province in the north.

The southwestern corner of Ethiopia is geographically part of the Nile basin of central Africa, and its Negroid peoples are called Nilotes.

Neither the white *shamma* of the highland Amharas nor

the color-drenched garments of the eastern Galla are to be found among the Nilotic peoples of Ilubabor and neighboring provinces. Among the cattle-herding Nuer tribes of Ilubabor, for example, married women wear breechcloths and little else, except for the usual adornments of beads, while other members of these tribes go unclad. Among the Anuak, another important Nilotic people of this region, both men and women wear short wraparound skirts, leaving the upper part of the body bare except for strands of necklaces. The women, especially, favor bracelets worn on both upper and lower arms and headbands that cut deeply into the flesh of the forehead. Some of the tribes rub their bodies with the ashes from their cookfires. The coating of ash is supposed to be an effective insect repellent.

The Anuak are mainly farmers. Their basic food crop is kafir corn, a grain-sorghum plant that is similar to American maize except that the kernels must be ground into a meal in order to be digestible when cooked. The Nuer trade some of their animal products for the grain and other farm products of the Anuak, and both tribal groups eat a boiled mush of kafir cornmeal as their staple food. The typical dwelling house of this region is a beehive-shaped hut, walled with cornstalks plastered with mud and roofed with thatch.

Most of the Negroid peoples of southwestern Ethiopia speak dialects of central Africa rather than the Amharic of the highlanders, the Arabic of the eastern coastal people, or the Galla and related Cushitic tongues of other Ethiopians. They follow ancient animistic religions and worship such objects as trees, mountains, animals, or stones, based on the belief that all things in nature have souls.

One of Ethiopia's very few navigable rivers, the crocodile-infested Baro, flows westward through Ilubabor Province to meet the White Nile in the Sudan. The village of Gambela is an important trading center on the river's banks. Roads are as scarce in this lush lowland as they are in the craggy highlands, so the people of the area journey on foot to Gambela to trade. Those who live along the Baro travel to Gambela by river in dugout canoes.

In contrast to the lush green of Kaffa and Ilubabor, Ethiopia's northwestern border with the Sudan is hot, low-lying desert country once again. These semiarid plains of western Eritrea Province are the home of nomadic Moslem peoples. One of the larger tribes is the Beni Amer, who herd

A child of one of the Negroid tribes of Ethiopia's southwest

camels and goats and keep some cattle. The Beni Amer follow the practice of stiffening their hair with mud or—as many primitive Ethiopian peoples do—with butter.

The highland region of the northwest is the site of Ethiopia's largest lake, Lake Tana, with an area of 1400 square miles. The lake is dotted with small islands, some of which contain churches and monasteries dating from the thirteenth century. The people who live along the shores fish the lake and paddle between shore points in slim curved boats made of bundles of papyrus and known as *tanquas.* Swimming is dangerous in Lake Tana due to the presence of bilharzia worms, which cause a serious parasitic disease.

Lake Tana is the source of outflow of Ethiopia's fabled Blue Nile River. The river flows for one thousand miles through northwestern Ethiopia and the eastern Sudan to join the White Nile at Khartoum, whence the combined waters of the Nile flow northward for another 1750 miles, through Egypt, into the Mediterranean. The Blue Nile is not a navigable river. If it were, it would have opened Ethiopia to the world, even in ancient times. Throughout the entire 470 miles of its flow within Ethiopia, the Blue Nile cannot even be followed on land. Its banks are steep, rugged, and twisting. Fed by mountain tributaries, the river descends stormily from Lake Tana and lashes its way westward cutting a deep and widening gorge. Only a few isolated villages are to be found on the shores of the Ethiopian Blue Nile. In places where the river does not boil with fierce rapids, it is a hippopotamus wallow and is infested with crocodiles. It is only when the Blue Nile approaches the desert borderland between Ethiopia and the Sudan that it begins to become navigable for small river craft.

Those early travelers and explorers who attempted to reach

The Blue Nile Falls spill out of Lake Tana in the highlands of the northwest.

the Ethiopian highlands by means of the Blue Nile waterway soon learned that progress was virtually impossible beyond the Sudan-Ethiopian borderland. One cannot help wondering what the history and present-day character of Ethiopia would be if the Blue Nile had served as an entry route to the slave traders of the sixteenth and seventeenth centuries, and to the European colonial powers of the eighteenth and nineteenth centuries.

As it is, the land of the lion, although locked away from the world until the present century, was able to maintain a unique freedom and independence on a continent that was otherwise destined to lie for long years under foreign domination and control.

II
YEARS OF ISOLATION

ETHIOPIANS ARE PROUD OF THEIR LONG HISTORY, WHICH they trace back to biblical times and which is firmly rooted in the legend of King Solomon and the Queen of Sheba. It is believed that Makeda, the Queen of Sheba, dwelt in Axum, today a holy city in Tigré Province, in the northern highlands.

Ethiopians tell the story this way:

Makeda was not only a beautiful woman, but she was also wise and longed to pay a visit to Solomon, the famous king of Judea. Messengers and presents were exchanged between the sovereigns and Makeda accepted King Solomon's invitation to visit him in the land of the Hebrews.

The queen was as much impressed with the king's wisdom and the luxury of his court as he was with her beauty. The king wanted very much to have Makeda as the mother of one of his children. But she steadfastly refused.

One day King Solomon made the queen promise that, should she take anything from his palace without his permission, she would immediately become his. That evening he had a very salty and spicy meal served and, as the king and his guests retired behind the curtains where their beds had been prepared, a tempting vase of clear water and a crystal cup were left in a prominent place.

About midnight, Makeda, tortured by thirst, dared to pour a cup of that fresh water for herself. Whereupon the king, who had been watching, came out from behind his curtain. "Aha," he said, "I caught you taking from my palace something which does not belong to you. Remember that which you promised."

After the Queen of Sheba returned to her own country, she bore King Solomon a son. When the child was old enough, the queen sent him to his father. King Solomon welcomed his son, saw to it that the boy's studies were completed, and later sent him back to Ethiopia with a present, the famous Tables of the Law of Moses. In time, Makeda's son became king of Ethiopia, with the name Menelik I.

These far-reaching events are believed to have taken place nearly one thousand years before the birth of Christ. The Tables of the Law of Moses, also known as the Ark of the Covenant, are said to rest to this day in the old Church of Saint Mary of Zion at Axum. Haile Selassie I, who became emperor of Ethiopia in 1930, is said to be the 225th ruler in the hereditary line that sprang from the union of King Solomon and the Queen of Sheba.

Historians, however, place the land of Sheba, also called Saba, in southern Arabia, across the Red Sea from Ethiopia. While Ethiopia may have been part of the Sabean empire at the time, it seems doubtful that the Queen of Sheba ruled from Axum.

The Church of Saint Mary of Zion at Axum, said to hold the Ark of the Covenant given to the Ethiopians by King Solomon

Nevertheless, archeologists have found evidences of a flourishing pre-Christian civilization at Axum. In recent years, ancient tombs have been uncovered that Ethiopians believe to be the graves of the Queen of Sheba and her son Menelik I. Nearby lie the ruins of a lavish stone palace of perhaps fifty rooms in which the queen is said to have lived. And a little farther off is an ancient reservoir, still in use by the people of Axum, known as the Bath of the Queen of Sheba.

From earliest times, the Red Sea coast was the principal means of access to Ethiopia. The ancient Egyptians, who had constructed a chain of canals linking the Nile Delta with the Red Sea, made expeditions to Ethiopian shores as early as 1500 years before the birth of Christ. They called the coastal region of Ethiopia the "land of Punt," and from it they brought back to Egypt slaves, cattle, animal skins, monkeys, ivory, and horn.

Still in pre-Christian times, Homer, the ninth-century Greek poet, and Herodotus, the fifth-century Greek historian, mentioned Ethiopia in their writings. In fact, it was the Greeks who gave Ethiopia its name.

Greek travelers reported that they had visited a land of "people with burnt faces." The Greek word for these dark-skinned inhabitants was *ethiopes.* In later centuries, Ethiopia came to be called Abyssinia, probably from the name of one of the early tribes that populated it, or from an Arabic word meaning many races or peoples. In modern times, the ancient Greek-given name—Ethiopia—has come into use again.

The story of Sheba's rule at Axum in the tenth century B.C. may be legend, but historical records tell us that by the first century A.D. Axum was the principal center of civilization in Ethiopia. Travelers and traders reached the city from the Red Sea port of Adulis. The overland journey was reported to take from eight to twelve days. As Axum lay near the northerly tip of the Ethiopian highlands, it was also a connecting point for caravans making the difficult overland journey between the Nile and the Red Sea.

Axum boasted a remarkable architecture. The famous steles, some of which are still standing today, were built in the third and early fourth centuries A.D. Although they are sometimes called obelisks, the Axum steles are not like the obelisks of ancient Egypt in contour or purpose. Tall, slender monuments, each one a slab of solid granite, the steles of pre-Christian Axum are believed to have been royal tombstones designed to house the spirits of the dead. Some were carved to represent skyscraperlike buildings with an imitation door at the bottom. The mounting stories above were carved with rows of "windows." Additional carvings on these granite columns represented building blocks of masonry and even the round ends of circular wooden beams. Such beams were used as crossbars in the actual construction of buildings in Ethiopia and southern Arabia at the time.

The largest of the Axum steles was thirteen stories high and over one hundred feet tall. There is little doubt that in its day it was the tallest monolith in the world. Today it

The standing stele of Axum, erected in the fourth century A.D.

lies fallen and broken on its original site. The largest standing stele, nine stories high in addition to its "ground floor," is seventy feet tall. It has an altarlike base with several deep cavities, probably for receiving the blood of animals sacrificed as offerings at the grave of the deceased. The fan-shaped stone apex of the fallen stele is carved with the sun-and-moon symbols of the Sabean religion, which was widely practiced in southern Arabia and Ethiopia at the time.

The material for the monuments must have been taken from the granite quarries that lay in the vicinity of Axum. It is believed that the steles were partially carved in the quarry, then cut free from the rock, further carved and shaped, then rolled on logs to the site where they were to be erected.

Some of the Axum steles were built during the early part of the reign of King Ezana, in the fourth century. Later Ezana became the first Christian king of Ethiopia. He was converted by two Syrian Christians, Frumentius and Aedisius, who had arrived at Axum during the reign of his father, King Ella Amida, and had been appointed tutors to the young prince.

Around the year 340, after he had ascended the throne, Ezana was baptized, and Christianity became the official religion. Saint Mary of Zion, believed to be the first Christian church in Ethiopia, was built after Ezana's conversion.

Many coins from Ezana's reign have been found. The earlier ones show the symbols of the old Sabean moon-and-star religion; the later ones show the Christian cross. These Ethiopian coins are believed to be the oldest coins in existence to bear this Christian symbol.

The Axumite kingdom flourished through the sixth century A.D. Under the Emperor Kaleb (514-542) and his son, Gebre-Maskal, the Ethiopians consolidated their Christian empire in southern Arabia, parts of which had already been conquered as early as the third century. But the golden age of Axum was drawing to a close, for the year 622 saw the birth of Islam, the Moslem religion, on the Arabian peninsula across the Red Sea.

At first, relations between the two religions were friendly, and the persecuted followers of the Prophet Mohammed who fled from cities in Arabia were given refuge at Axum. Later, however, as Islam gathered strength, the coastal region of Ethiopia was overrun with newly converted militant Moslems. Conflicts between Christians and Moslems arose and increased in violence. The Ethiopian highland regions were soon cut off, isolated, and Axum sank into a state of decline.

Today a quiet town of about 20,000 people, Axum has re-

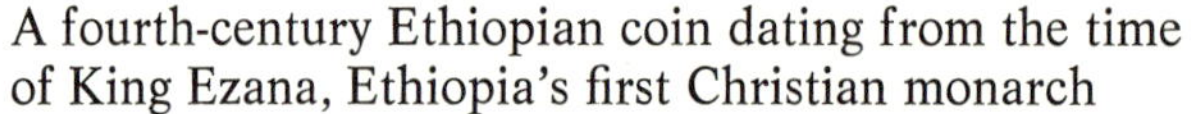

A fourth-century Ethiopian coin dating from the time of King Ezana, Ethiopia's first Christian monarch

tained its importance as the "holy city" of Ethiopia and remains the traditional coronation site of the Ethiopian emperors.

Centuries of chaos followed the dissolution of the Axumite Kingdom. In 1137 a new dynasty known as the Zagwé, not descended from Solomon and Sheba, established itself at Roha, which lay far to the south of Axum, deep among the jagged peaks of the central highlands.

Here, in the late twelfth and early thirteenth centuries, the Zagwé king, Lalibela, built a series of churches to serve as the core of his "new Jerusalem." The eleven churches in the immediate vicinity of Lalibela (as Roha soon came to be called) are monoliths, carved out of solid rock.

One of the monolithic churches of Lalibela, hewn from a mountain of solid rock

The rock-cut Church of Saint George, at Lalibela, which rests in a pit 40 feet deep and is entered by an underground passage at its base

The churches had to be shaped by hewing downward through mountains of stone, rather than built from the bottom up as in ordinary construction. Their exteriors were completely finished, with porches, columns, roof carvings, and other decorations. Each church was then freed from its rock surroundings by digging an encircling trench at its base. The interiors were then hollowed out and these, too, were fully developed, with columns, arches, and low-relief carvings.

King Lalibela lived from about 1150 to 1220. The churches he built are "living churches," for nearly all are in use during the many holy days of the Ethiopian religious year. King Lalibela is today revered as a saint in Ethiopia, even though his dynasty was outside the Solomonic line.

To the many pilgrims who travel by foot for days and weeks to attend services in this remote and primitive place, Lalibela still represents a "new Jerusalem." Lalibela village itself is a small community of about 3000 Christian Amharas,

The two-story stone *tukuls* of Lalibela village

who live in two-story *tukuls* built of local stone and capped with conical roofs of thatch.

The rule of the Zagwé dynasty came to an end in 1270, when the king was forced to give up the throne to a nobleman of the Solomonic line. The restoration of the dynasty of Solomon was the work of Tekla Haimanot, an Ethiopian statesman, who later was elevated to sainthood because he acquired much land for the church from the new king.

In the period that followed, the most notable ruler was Zar'a Ya'kob, who ruled from 1434 to 1468 and was considered by many the greatest king since Ezana, one thousand years earlier. A devout Christian, he strengthened the position of the church in Ethiopia, firmly united church and state, controlled the Moslems, and expanded his domain.

In Europe, during the fourteenth century, a curious story began to circulate: somewhere in Africa, or possibly in Asia, ruled a Christian monarch of great wealth named Prester John. Eventually European attention began to focus on Ethiopia as the probable abode of Prester John.

After the Portuguese nagivator Bartolomeu Dias rounded the Cape of Good Hope in 1488, Ethiopia came within reach of European sea expeditions. In 1520, the Portuguese king sent a diplomatic mission to Ethiopia. The party made its way inland to the central highlands and remained until 1526.

The reports brought back to Portugal by members of the mission were somewhat disappointing. Hope of discovering the land of Prester John had been abandoned. The mission found instead a beleaguered Ethiopian monarch, entrenched in a savage landscape from which he made constant forays against the Moslem hordes that threatened to overrun his limited Christian domain.

The year after the departure of the Portuguese, in 1527, the Moslem *jihad,* or holy war, began in earnest in Ethiopia. Its leader was Imam Ahmed ibn Ibrahim al-Ghazi, from the Moslem stronghold city of Harar in the east. To the Amharas and Tigreans of the Ethiopian highlands, this scourge of Christianity was known as Ahmed Gran. *Gran* is the Amharic word for "left-handed."

During the next sixteen years, Gran ravaged central and northern Ethiopia, looting, burning property, and destroying churches everywhere with almost unabated ferocity. He had the backing and support of Moslems—the Somalis and other nomads of eastern Ethiopia and the Ottoman Turks, who were then extending their empire in Europe, Asia, and Africa.

As the Christian forces felt themselves weakening, the Ethiopian king, Lebna Dengal, began to ask the Portuguese for help against the Moslems. Lebna Dengal died in 1540, but in 1541 a Portuguese force finally arrived in Ethiopia.

It was led by Christopher da Gama, son of Vasco da Gama, the Portuguese navigator who had been the first European to reach India by sea, in 1498.

The young da Gama tracked down Gran and his people, but was killed in battle along with many of his men. The remaining Portuguese and Ethiopian forces, led by the Ethiopian emperor Claudius, finally killed Gran near Lake Tana in 1543.

It was during the period of devastation following the long Moslem campaign that the Galla migrated northward and swept over the Ethiopian heartland, settling in large numbers among the exhausted and demoralized Christians of Ethiopia.

An even more serious threat to Ethiopia's centuries-old form of Christianity was the arrival from Portugal, in the latter half of the century, of a group of Jesuit priests and monks whose mission was to convert the Ethiopian Christians to the Roman Catholic faith.

The Spanish Jesuit, Pero Paez, came in 1603 and was able to convert the Emperor Za Dengal. However, when Paez died in 1622, a later Emperor, Susenyos, gave up his efforts to convert his unwilling subjects. Pressured to return to Ethiopia's own Coptic branch of Christianity, Susenyos expelled all Jesuits in 1632 and gave up the throne to his son, Fasil (or Fasiladas).

The experience with the Jesuits left the Ethiopian people with a keen distrust of foreigners. It was clear that in inviting the Portuguese to help them against the Moslems, the Ethiopians had simply invited evil to fight evil. Henceforward they tended to view all outsiders with wariness if not hostility.

In 1636, intending to wipe out the memories of the troubled years that had preceded his reign, the new king

Seventeenth-century castles in the palace compound of King Fasil at Gondar

Fasil moved the capital of Ethiopia to Gondar, a site forty miles north of Lake Tana across a broad, fertile plain. Situated at an elevation of 7000 feet, with a mountain barrier to the north, Gondar enjoyed a handsome setting and a fine climate.

There the king built a large palace compound, surrounded by a twelve-gated wall. Although most Portuguese had been banished from the country by this time, the turreted and battlemented stone castles of Gondar, with their balconies, archways, and decorative details, show an unmistakable Portuguese-Moorish influence.

In addition to the impressive main palace of King Fasil, a library, theater, banquet hall, three churches, and two other palaces were built in the compound in later years. Some were

Fasiladas' Bath, where the royal bathing parties took place in the water-filled pool

erected before the death of Fasil in 1667; others were added by his successors to the imperial throne at Gondar, among them Yasu I (1682-1706), known as the Great. The palace compound also included a group of lion cages, as the Ethiopian emperors traditionally kept representatives of the king of beasts near them as pets, mascots, and symbols of their power.

Churches abounded in the new capital. One of the most notable is the church of Debre Berhan Selassie ("Trinity of the Mountain Light"), with its ceiling of great-eyed benevolent angels' faces painted in rich, glowing earth colors.

Gondar in its golden age was Ethiopia's most culturally advanced capital to date, a thriving center of poetry, music, manuscript art, architecture, and commerce, with a population of 80,000. But Gondar was not the political center of Ethiopia.

Unification of the country, even of the Amhara and Tigrean Christian peoples, had never really been achieved. In the past, capitals had been shifted frequently and many an Ethiopian monarch had been forced to accept an itinerant way of life to try to hold his people together. It was quite common for the king or emperor to be constantly on the move, traveling about the country with his armies, making policy and directing his warrior-generals from a temporary throne in a hastily pitched royal tent. Revolts by petty feudal chieftains were frequent and had to be put down repeatedly. The establishment of the permanent Ethiopian capital at Gondar increased the difficulty of ruling.

By 1770, when the independent Scots explorer, James Bruce, visited Gondar, the country was once again in a state of deep turmoil. The king was virtually the pawn of his vizier, Ras Mikael Suhul, a Tigrean noble. Feudal warfare ravaged the countryside. The armies of the Ethiopian chieftains were constantly at war with one another or against the ever-present threat of Islam. Bruce reported that the soldiers even plundered their own villages and indulged frequently in their customary warrior-banquets of raw meat, carved from the flanks of living cattle, and *tej,* an alcoholic drink prepared from fermented honey.

Bruce remained in Ethiopia for two years, visiting the true source of the Blue Nile in a highland bog some distance from Lake Tana. Known in Ethiopia as the Little Abbai, this river flows into Lake Tana, where it appears to lose itself. He also visited and described the Blue Nile Falls, the point at which the river, here called the Big Abbai, tumbles out of Lake Tana into the pools and riverbed below. His tales of the river source and the Blue Nile Falls and his accounts of eighteenth-century life in the Ethiopian highlands were considered exaggerations when he returned to Great Britain, however, and were little believed.

Today Gondar is a small but progressive city of 32,000 inhabitants. Its ruined castles and many churches reflect the glories of its vanished past.

Ethiopia entered the nineteenth century as a still primitive land where strife and chaos reigned. Even the European powers, busily engaged in the African-colony race, seemed to take no notice of this unyielding place with its inhospitable terrain. No leader had emerged who was strong enough to subdue, unify, and modernize Ethiopia.

Until the year 1800, Ethiopia was closed away from the world. In this isolation there developed the traditions, customs, and the patterns of everyday life that were to persist into the twentieth century.

III
EVERYDAY LIFE

WHAT IS IT LIKE TO BE BORN AN AMHARA PEASANT and grow up in the highlands, to live in a *tukul,* to follow the same life patterns as one's parents and their parents before them?

Beneath the thatched roof of the *tukul,* the family and often the animals as well live clustered together. The simplest home consists of one room. Its hearth is merely a pit in the earthen floor. It has no chimney, no windows, and only a single low doorway, so that the room is dark and smoke-filled. Lining the curving walls are earthen benches, which at night are covered with hides or sheepskins for sleeping.

To build a round hut, the peasant begins with a ring of slender tree trunks or peeled saplings driven into the ground. The stakes are placed close together, for they must hold the plaster of clayey mud, usually mixed with chopped grass, that forms both the inner and outer walls. Rafters and a pole in the center of the hut hold up the cone-shaped roof. The pointed top of the roof is sometimes decorated with an ostrich egg, from which the contents have been drained, or a hollow dried gourd. Such ornaments represent the idea of

Tukuls and tin-roofed huts in a small Amhara village, showing frameworks of peeled saplings

eternal life through resurrection. Or the roof point may simply be finished off with a topknot of grass tufts.

A more prosperous family may build a large *tukul* with two circular rooms, one within the other. These are formed by putting up an interior circular partition of stone, wood, or mud. The animals can then be kept in the outer, ring-shaped room. Often the Amhara homestead consists of several small buildings, including one or more for animals, storage, and utility purposes. There may also be a guest *tukul* for entertaining visitors and one for a newly married son and his wife to live in.

In the highland towns and cities, the modest huts of the poor often have roofs of tin rather than thatch, and their

Grinding *teff* with a hand stone rubbed across a large stone with a hollow to catch the ground grain

shape may be rectangular instead of round. In the provinces of Tigré and Eritrea in the north, even the mud-and-thatch houses of the countryside frequently have rectangular shapes and flatter roofs, as the rainfall is lighter in the north.

The furnishings of the home are simple: several three-legged wooden stools, a small serving table for the Ethiopian one-dish meals, a large flat stone with a hollow in it, on which grain is ground into flour. There is a *metad,* an earthenware or iron disc for baking *injera,* the Ethiopian pancake-bread, as well as cooking pots and water jugs. As the floor space is so limited in the *tukul,* hooks are driven into the walls for hanging household tools, kitchen utensils, garments, and bed coverings.

The workday begins well before dawn in the typical highland home. The mother is the first up, for she must grind *teff,* or millet flour, for the breakfast *injera,* blow the embers of last night's fire into flame, bake the *injera,* and heat the spicy sauce that is eaten with it.

After breakfast the children are sent off to the fields and hillsides to graze the family sheep, goats, and cattle. If the family lives within reach of a village or church school, some of the children may be sent off to their studies.

The father of the family often begins his day with a brief period of prayer or religious reading. After he has washed and eaten, he goes about his tasks. Depending on the season, he may be planting crops or harvesting them. To prepare his fields for planing, the Ethiopian farmer uses a primitive, ox-driven wooden plow with a single iron blade. Ripe grain is cut with a sickle, then trampled beneath the hooves of oxen to separate the grain or seeds from the husks, and finally tossed high into the breeze with a wooden fork to separate the grain from the chaff.

At noon the father may return home for his midday meal, or his wife may take it to him in the fields. The children stay with the roaming and grazing animals throughout the day and eat a lunch of cold pancake-bread, roasted grain seeds, or cooked dried beans.

The mother is kept busy at home. She must gather the animal dung or wood that she will use for her cookfire, fetch water from the spring, sweep the hut, spin and weave, cook a fresh batch of sauce or a stew to be eaten with the *injera* at the evening meal, and prepare the Ethiopian home-brewed beer known as *talla.* She must also tend to the younger children and nurse the baby, who goes about with her most of the day strapped to her back.

The close of day sees the family gathered in the *tukul* for the evening meal. *Talla* is served to the father and to the older sons. The children are put to bed one by one, after having washed their feet and said their evening prayers. The father retires and, lastly, the mother. The animals, too, have bedded down. Outside the tiny homestead, there is only the stillness of the vast African night.

The food customs of Ethiopia have been handed down from generation to generation and have seen little change, even in modern times. *Injera* is the bread of most people. It requires no bake oven and can be cooked quickly over an open fire. It is usually made from *teff* but occasionally can also be prepared from barley or other flour, to which water

Left: A painting showing a mother pouring *injera* batter onto a *metad,* making a special small-sized *injera* to please her child
Right: A *masob* and tray on which *injera* is served

and a fermented yeast mixture is added. The *metad* is balanced atop three stones over a hot fire and the *injera* batter poured onto the disclike pan, starting from the outside and working toward the center. A cover is then placed over the *metad* and the *injera* bakes by steaming in only a few minutes.

The finished *injera,* which may be as large as two feet in diameter, ranges from pale gray to brown, depending on the flour used. Spongy, with tiny air holes, and about one-quarter inch thick, it has a bland, slightly sour grain flavor.

Warm or cold, the *injera* is arranged in layers and served on a tray atop a small, round, portable serving table woven of straw, resembling a tall basket. This is called a *masob.* A sharp-flavored reddish sauce or stew, prepared with onions and peppery spices, is ladled over the *injera.* In Amharic this sauce is called *wat;* in Tigrinya it is *zegeni.* The everyday *wat* of the poor peasant contains no meat, but on special occasions it becomes a stew with chunks of chicken, lamb, tripe, beef, or ground beef in it. *Doro wat* is a "hot" chicken stew with whole hard-cooked eggs in it. Pork is almost never eaten in Ethiopia, as it is considered taboo by Ethiopian Christians and is also strictly forbidden by the Moslem religion.

At an Ethiopian meal, the hands are washed before and after eating. During the meal itself, the *injera* serves as the plate, napkin, fork, spoon, and knife, as pieces of *injera* are torn off with the fingers and used to scoop up the sauce and its morsels of meat and vegetables. Only the right hand is used in eating from the *masob.*

The Ethiopian beer is brewed from barley or other grains and is fermented with the leaves from a shrub or tree called the *gesho.* A brew of home-made *talla* takes about ten days until it is ready for drinking. The beer is dark brown and not very intoxicating. *Tej,* which is made from honey fermented with *gesho* leaves, is served on more important occasions. *Tej* can be sweet and winelike or strongly alcoholic, depending on the degree of fermentation.

In the old days, when parasite-infested raw meat was widely eaten in Ethiopia, it was washed down with strong *tej* in the belief that the alcohol would kill the parasites. *Berberi,* a powdered spice made from very sharp dried peppers, was also eaten with raw meat for this reason. *Berberi* is an ingredient of *wat,* along with herbs and other spices.

Peas, beans, chick-peas, and lentils play an important part in the daily diet. A meatless Lenten dish called *salgo* is prepared by grinding these legumes and stewing them with water and spices. With the exception of tomatoes and peppers in season, few fresh vegetables and almost no fresh fruits are found in the diet of most Ethiopians, particularly in the highlands.

Ethiopians seem not to have a sweet tooth either, although sugarcane stalks, when available, are sometimes chewed or sucked. A teaspoonful of honey may be stirred into a small cup of Ethiopian coffee. For ordinary nibbling, youngsters enjoy a handful of *kolo,* a mixture of roasted whole kernels of barley, corn, or other seed grains. Another treat is *dabo kolo,* an unsweetened flour dough rolled into pencil-thin strips, then pinched off into tiny bits and baked. *Kolo* means grain, so *dabo kolo* means "flour" grain.

The etiquette of eating is strictly observed at the Ethiopian table. In peasant families, the father is always served first. Children eat afterward or may stand during the meal and have bits of *injera* and *wat* placed directly in their mouths by the adults or by their older brothers.

It is also a tradition of Ethiopian hospitality for the host or hostess to place a fold of *injera* containing a particularly tasty morsel of *wat* directly into the mouth of the guest. Refusal is unthinkable. Such an offering is called a *gursha.*

In the past there have been no hotels or wayside inns in Ethiopia. Even casual travelers are fed and given a bed in a private home. If there is no guest *tukul,* the visitor will be offered a place on the floor, made up of a mound of grass or straw covered with a hide.

When a guest is expected, his host walks a considerable distance to meet him and escort him home. Immediately upon arrival, the guest is offered *kolo* and generous amounts of *talla* or *tej* or coffee. Later, or the next day, when the guest leaves, his host accompanies him well along on his way and watches with concern until he is out of sight.

The peasant highlander attends the weekly market that is held in his vicinity, even though it may lie at a considerable distance from his isolated homestead. It is not unusual for the trip, which is usually made on foot, to take nearly half a day's journey each way.

When he is traveling anywhere, a man almost always takes a staff, or *dula.* He ordinarily carries the *dula* behind his back, braced across his shoulder blades, one end grasped in each hand. At other times, the *dula* is carried slanted across the shoulder like a rifle. It is helpful for beating off small animals and making his way through the underbrush or across difficult terrain. At times, a man may even prop it under his arm and use it as a crutch while standing on one leg and resting the other, just as the Ethiopian priests do with their prayer sticks during the long church services.

At the highland markets the peasant can buy or barter for

Ethiopian foot-travelers, one carrying a *dula*

onions, spices, salt, grains, chickens, eggs, honey, beeswax, cotton, pottery and ironware, or a load of firewood. The local people often exchange their wares. A widow woman comes to the market bent double under her load of firewood, which she will barter for some scoopfuls of grain, a handful of onions, and the few spices that will see her through her meager meals for the next week.

At the market money changes hands mainly in transactions with vendors of metals and other goods that are manufactured or goods that are sold by peddlers who have come a long

A big-city marketplace: the grain market at Asmara

distance. The average highlander is still suspicious of paper money, as it seems to have no lasting value. A coin still treasured in Ethiopia is the Maria Theresa silver thaler, issued by the Austrian Empire in 1780. Of almost pure silver, these foreign coins were legal tender in Ethiopia until the 1940's. The Ethiopian national currency today consists of paper dollars and mixed-metal quarters, dimes, and smaller coins. The dollar was chosen as the unit of currency to avoid confusion with the British East African and Italian currencies common in Ethiopia at the time and also because the new monetary system was developed with the help of a large loan from the United States government.

In the towns and cities there are daily markets. In Addis Ababa, local people and peasants from the surrounding hills congregate at the Mercato, reputed to be the largest marketplace in Africa. Barter is less common here, but haggling over prices is the order of the day whether the bargained-for item is a paper twist of ground spice, a twelve-foot roll of linoleum, or a warrior's shield of hippopotamus hide.

The rows of arcaded shops border on busy passageways crammed with animals, horn-honking vehicles, and laughing and arguing shoppers and tradesmen. A common feature of the Mercato, as of the markets in other towns, is the tailors who sit at their treadle-operated sewing machines in the shade of the arcade or in a small grove of trees. The shopper who buys a length of cloth at the market can bring it home

Weighing locally grown cotton on a hand-held balance scale in the marketplace at Axum

as a shirt, coat, or trousers, for it will be quickly and cheaply converted into the desired garment by these on-the-spot tailors.

Families tend to be large in Ethiopia. Sometimes there are as many as seventeen or eighteen children. According to Ethiopian Christian custom, boy babies are baptized forty days after birth, girls on the eightieth day. At this time they are given their first names, although some superstitious parents give the child a temporary name and withhold the true name until the child is well into the first year of life. They fear that if the child's name is known, evil spirits will seek him out and destroy him, and their superstition is rooted in fact, for the infant mortality rate is very high—in rural areas as high as one child out of every five.

Ethiopians do not have family second names. A child takes

Marketplace tailors at treadle-operated sewing machines converting lengths of cloth into garments for waiting customers

its father's first name as its second name. If a boy's father's first name was Hagos, and the boy is given the name Yohannes, he is then known throughout life as Yohannes Hagos.

Many Ethiopian names have meanings. Hagos, for example, means "joy"; a girl might be called Hagosa. Yohannes, however, is the Amharic for John, just as Maryam is Mary. These, of course, are biblical names.

There are many compound names in Ethiopia. Gebre means "slave of" or "servant of," so the given name Gebre-Mikael is really "servant of Michael." Wolde-Giorgis is "son of George"; Habte-Amanuel is "gift of Emanuel." A girl or boy whose father has one of these names will then be called Hagosa Gebre-Mikael or Yohannes Wolde-Giorgis. Ethiopians are always addressed by their first names with the prefix of *ato* (Mr.), *woizero* (Mrs.), or *woizerit* (Miss): Ato Yohannes, Woizero Hagosa, Woizerit Maryam.

During the first years of their lives, Ethiopian children are coddled and indulged, remaining close to their mothers even after they have grown much too heavy to be carried on their backs in a protective shrouding of white cotton cloth. But by the time the Amhara peasant child is three to four years old, it begins to have small duties such as gathering twigs and branches for the fire, feeding the chickens, and frightening birds and small animals away from the harvested grain.

Boys start going out each day with the grazing herds by the time they are six, while girls remain at home learning to spin, carry water, and grind grain by rubbing it up and back on the grindstone with a small hand-held stone. The lives of the peasant children become increasingly serious and purposeful as they grow older. They have very few toys and play

An Amhara child carrying her baby sister on her back in traditional fashion

simple games: a kind of hopscotch, with lines drawn in the dirt with a stick, for younger children; wrestling and war and hunting games for the boys. Girls may have dolls made of straw and rags.

Although the high spirits of youth are not completely suppressed, there is no "rebellion," no "youth culture." Girls are usually married at twelve or thirteen, boys by their late teens or early twenties. The Ethiopian peasant boy must learn how to work the land, and often by his middle teens he has a small parcel of land that he farms all on his own.

Most marriages are still arranged by the parents, but frequently a boy will see a girl who appeals to him at a church festival or other local gathering and will then ask for parental approval of the match. Once the families of the prospective bride and groom have agreed on the amount of land, livestock, household and personal goods each will contribute to the new couple, the marriage contract is drawn up. Despite the strong position of the church in Ethiopian life, most marriages are performed in a brief, simple civil ceremony. Only priests, deacons, and extremely pious couples are married in a religious ceremony. Church marriages are binding for life, but civil marriages can be dissolved with very little formality, so divorce is quite common even among the traditional peasant families.

The wedding ceremony, whether civil or religious, is marked by a bout of feasting, with the bride's family and the groom's family offering separate celebrations. The newly married couple then settles temporarily in the home of the groom's parents where they may spend a few months or even a few years. Often they will make their home in a small *tukul* on the boy's parents' homestead until they are ready to set up a separate home of their own.

Soon children begin to arrive, and the lives of the married couple slip into the same patterns their parents have known. The daily round is broken by the same predictable events: market days, trips to the local law courts to settle the perpetual squabbles over land rights and ownership, religious holidays, and family events such as christenings, weddings, and funerals.

Parasitic diseases, malnutrition, tuberculosis, and other illnesses take the lives of Ethiopians of all ages. The average life-span is only 36.1 years, a shocking figure. Yet many do live into their seventies, and these elders are much respected for the experience and wisdom that are the gift of years. Old age is a condition that most Ethiopians aspire to rather than dread.

When death comes, there is much loud lamenting. The family or neighbors wash the body and prepare it for burial in a white shroud. Like the Hebrews, the Ethiopian Christians bury their dead as soon as possible and then enter a week of intense mourning. During this period friends and relatives visit daily with the bereaved family. Forty days after the death a special mass is held at the church, and this is followed by a great banquet.

The single most important factor introducing changes into the traditional patterns of peasant life is the growing number of government schools, particularly in the cities, towns, and larger villages.

The animals may still live with the family under a roof of tin, as they do even in the very center of Addis Ababa, and the father may still go off each day to work a patch of land in the nearby countryside. But the herd boys of the remote hills are gradually becoming schoolboys. Their sisters are not far behind in joining them in the classroom.

As new worlds of knowledge and opportunity open to young people, the old traditions are being shaken. The school begins to take over the role of the parent, the family group, the tribe, and even the church. The child studies English, which is compulsory in all government schools. He encounters foreign-trained and even foreign-born teachers. He is encouraged to pursue further schooling, with free tuition and with subsidies offered if he must live away from home to attend.

For the first time choices are being offered to a generation of peasant-born children. Adult responsibilities may not be thrust upon young people in their adolescent years, which may instead be taken up with study and activities similar to those of Western youth. Marriage may be delayed, and when it comes it does not always follow the established patterns.

Just as Ethiopia resisted the influences of the outside world for centuries, so the peasantry will resist influences that threaten to break down the traditional way of life. But the first signs of change can decidedly be seen, and a gap is beginning to open between the generations in Ethiopia's peasant society.

IV
RELIGION AND HOLIDAYS

THE ETHIOPIAN CHRISTIAN CHURCH, WITH ITS DEmanding rituals, its numerous fast days, and its imposing feast days, strongly dominates the lives of most Ethiopian Christians. Although only about half of Ethiopia's 25 million people are Christians, it is estimated that there are 18,000 churches in Ethiopia and 250,000 Christian clergymen.

The form of Christianity that the Ethiopians adopted in the fourth century is called Monophysitism. It is based on the belief that the divine and human natures of Christ are one. In 451 A.D., the Council of Chalcedon denounced the Monophysite doctrine as a heresy, but the Monophysite Church continued to flourish in Ethiopia, Egypt, Syria, and Armenia. In Egypt, Monophysite Christians are called Copts.

Until 1949, the patriarch of the Egyptian Coptic Church served as the head of the Ethiopian Monophysite Church as well. Each time the old archbishop of Ethiopia died, the Egyptian patriarch would appoint a new Egyptian prelate to be sent to Ethiopia, where he would live out his life as the *abuna,* or principal church official. Among the main functions of the *abuna* were the ordaining of priests and bishops and the crowning of Ethiopian emperors.

After 1949, Ethiopian bishops elected their own archbishop, and in 1959 the status of the Ethiopian head-of-church was raised to that of patriarch. The Ethiopian Monophysite Church is considerably larger than the Egyptian Coptic Church, for there are fewer than three million Christians in predominantly Islamic Egypt.

The Ethiopian priest, or *kes,* has often begun his training while a small boy attending a village church school. Most pupils learn the rudiments of religious reading and some writing and then drop away from school. The student who shows promise may continue with his religious studies. He must learn the scriptures and all phases of church liturgy, and he must learn to read the old manuscripts, which are written in Ghe'ez.

Ghe'ez is a Cushitic-Semitic language, probably a mixture of an ancient Ethiopian tongue and a southern Arabian dialect. It is sometimes called Ethiopic. It was the official spoken and written tongue of the Axumite Kingdom. Later, like Latin, new languages developed from it and Ghe'ez itself became a dead language. Some scholars say that Amhara and Tigrinya are to Ghe'ez what French and Italian are to Latin.

Manuscripts written in Ghe'ez, on fine goatskin or lambskin and often beautifully illustrated, have provided a great body of religious literature dating from the time of King Ezana. It was not until the nineteenth century, when printing presses were set up in Ethiopia, that books began to be written in Amharic.

While most Ethiopians do not read or understand Ghe'ez, it is still the language in which church services are conducted, and hand-written manuscripts in Ghe'ez are still being produced in Ethiopian monasteries.

While he is studying for the priesthood, a boy may serve as a deacon in the church. He assists at the Mass and marches in the processions on the various holy days. Often religious students live in the meanest huts and feed themselves solely by begging, while devoting nearly all their time to their studies.

The candidate for the priesthood must remain chaste through his adolescent years, for chastity is often the measure of a person's eligibility for attending Mass and taking Communion. He may marry, but his wife must be above reproach,

A boy preparing for the priesthood serves as a deacon in the church and assists the white-turbanned priest

and the marriage must take place in church. At the marriage ceremony the bride and groom take Communion together while standing beneath a single *shamma* held above their heads, in a tradition similar to that of the Hebrews.

Preparation for the priesthood may take as many as twelve years of study, after which time the student is ordained as a priest by the *abuna*. He now wears the white turban of his office, and he is able to conduct the Mass. He is permitted to enter the room known as the Holy of Holies, and he may handle the *tabot*.

The *tabot* is a carved rectangular tablet of stone or wood that represents the Ark of the Covenant, or the Tables of the Law of Moses, which Menelik I is believed to have brought back to Axum as the gift of his father, King Solomon.

The *tabot,* which rests within the church in a cubicle or inner room, the Holy of Holies, is the object that gives the church building its sanctity. The *tabot* is desecrated if it is seen undraped or touched by a lay person or by a priest who has not observed the proper period of fasting before or is not in a state of purity. The *tabot* is kept covered at all times but is taken from the Holy of Holies during church processions and for longer periods of time on certain holy days.

The Ethiopian priest is deeply respected. He carries a long-handled cross of silver, iron, brass, or wood, which people stop to touch with their foreheads and then kiss with great reverence. This Coptic cross is similar to the Greek cross. It has four arms of equal length and is quite ornately carved. Near the base of the handle there is a flat rectangular slab that rests across the handle and represents the *tabot.* The priest usually also carries that mark of the Ethiopian gentleman, an ivory-handled fly whisk of horsehair or monkey fur.

The life of the Ethiopian priest is relatively comfortable.

A priest's wooden cross with the rectangular slab at the base that represents the *tabot*

He may do some farming on his own, but he also receives a small salary from the church and many gifts and donations of money, food, and other goods from his parishioners. If a priest's wife dies, he must leave the priesthood. He may marry and still maintain his connection with the church by taking more religious studies in order to become a *dabtara*.

The *dabtara* holds a special place in the world of Ethiopian Christianity. He is a mixture of cantor, scribe, scholar, and medicine man. His office is not ordained by the *abuna* or any other religious leader, his position in the church is loosely defined, and he may receive his support from any number of religious or lay sources.

As he is not a holy person and may even have been divorced and remarried, the *dabtara* may not enter the Holy of Holies. However, he is almost indispensable to church ritual. He leads the choir and the chants and religious dances that are a vital part of the holy day observances. He has had more

Priests and *dabtaras* carrying processional crosses at a religious ceremony

years of study than the average priest, possibly twenty or thirty, so he is an expert at Ghe'ez and has a thorough knowledge of the scriptures. He interprets religious works, composes religious poetry, and often teaches in a church school. He is an expert in calligraphy and in the preparation of parchments for manuscripts and scrolls.

The *dabtara* wields great influence, too, because he has special knowledge of the arts of black magic. Many Ethiopian Christians are highly superstitious. They fear the evil eye, make secret "protection" pacts with the devil, and believe that spirits known as *zar* can cause the birth of defective children, transmit contagious diseases, and inflict madness.

The *dabtara* knows the proper herbs and incantations for dealing with illnesses, the evil eye, and other troubles. Many Ethiopians wear small cylindrical metal cases at their throats. These contain tightly rolled scrolls with magic spells written on them that have been specially composed by a *dabtara* to protect the wearer from a particular illness or evil happening.

Monks form another branch of the Ethiopian Christian clergy. While most live in monasteries, there are many hermit monks, both male and female, who live at the barest subsistence level in remote and inaccessible places. Others live as wanderer or pilgrim monks, subsisting off charity.

Ethiopia's principal monastery is that of Debra Libanos. Its chief, called the *ichegé,* is appointed by the emperor and is the spiritual leader of all the monks in Ethiopia. His command, however, is secondary to that of the *abuna.* Debra Libanos was founded by Saint Tekla Haimanot, who brought the Zagwé dynasty to an end and restored the Solomonic line in 1270.

A monk with the crown of Emperor Yasu I
from the treasure of Saint Mary of Zion

All Ethiopian monks must practice celibacy and renounce all worldly concerns. Monks are not ordained by the *abuna:* monkhood is conferred by the head of the particular monastery. Priests whose wives have died and who do not wish to remarry may become monks, and they often choose this way of life.

Many Ethiopian monasteries were built atop steep cliffs and were the repositories of precious manuscripts and other important religious objects during the ravages of Ahmed Gran in the sixteenth century.

Debre Damo is one of the best known and most intriguing of these clifftop monasteries. Its one hundred and fifty monks live on the flat summit of a sheer-faced mountain of rock that must be ascended by a leather rope. It is supposed to have

An Ethiopian priest entering the twelfth-century rock-cut Church of Abba Libanos at Lalibela

been founded as early as the sixth century, although its church is believed to date from the ninth or tenth century. According to legend, the first holy men to dwell on Debre Damo reached the top with the help of a huge serpent that was commanded by the Lord to uncoil its body and serve as a climbing rope. Women and female animals are not admitted to Debre Damo.

The island monasteries of Lake Tana served additionally as safe deposits for precious religious treasures and manuscripts.

Women are also not permitted to enter the very holy old Church of Saint Mary of Zion at Axum, built at the time of King Fasil in 1655. The reason given is that a woman—the

A Lenten procession circling the new
Church of Saint Mary of Zion at Axum

non-Christian Queen Judith—is said to have destroyed the churches of Axum in the tenth century. The old Saint Mary, like the original fourth century church that preceded it, is rectangular. Today a new Church of Saint Mary of Zion stands quite near the old church. Built in 1965 in a rotunda style, this church is open for worship to both men and women.

Most churches of central Ethiopia follow the building style of the *tukul* and are round. The round church is usually divided into concentric circles inside, with the Holy of Holies located in the core of the structure. The next circle is for those who are permitted to take Communion. These are usually pious Christians, who have been married in a religious ceremony, or young children. Once they have reached adolescence, few Ethiopians are permitted to take Communion again. Also, the sacraments of confirmation, confession, matrimony, and extreme unction are not considered mandatory in the Ethiopian Christian Church, while baptism and holy orders are.

The outermost circle of the round church is for the use of general worshippers. Men and women are separated. All worshippers must remove their shoes before entering the church. The area just outside the church is reserved for those Christians who have not fasted or are otherwise impure and who are therefore barred from entering the church. Often they stand clinging to the outside wall while the Mass is being performed within.

The more elaborate round churches sometimes take on an octagonal shape such as that of the Giorgis or Saint George Church in Addis Ababa, which was built in 1896 and where Emperor Haile Selassie was crowned in 1930. Most Ethiopian churches are topped by an eight-armed cross. The equal-length arms of the cross are joined together by a lacing pattern of decorative design that symbolizes eternity and infinity.

Saturdays and Sundays are both considered Sabbath days in the Ethiopian Church, and Christians perform no field work or other strenuous labor on those days. Wednesdays and Fridays are weekly fast days. No food or drink may be taken before noon, and the single meal which is then eaten, at midday or in the evening, must consist of vegetarian foods only.

The Lenten fast, which is eight weeks long on the Ethiopian Church calendar, is the most severe hardship. Fasting must be observed on all weekdays during Lent. Eating before noon is allowed only on Saturdays and Sundays. The food eaten throughout Lent may include no meats, meat fats, eggs, fish, or dairy products. Other sustained fasting periods take place at Advent and before the Feast of the Assumption. Devout Christians may fast as many as 165 days a year, while priests and other clergy must fast 250 days out of every 365. Even children begin to observe the fasts by the time they are six or seven.

The Ethiopian calendar is unique. Due to a different numbering of the years since the birth of Christ, the official calendar is seven years and eight months behind the Gregorian calendar that is used throughout most of the Western world today. In Ethiopia, the year 1963 began on September 11, 1970, and ended on September 10, 1971. While the Ethiopian year consists of 365 days, it has thirteen months—twelve months of thirty days each, and a final, thirteenth month of five days (six days in leap year). The first month of the Ethiopian year is Maskarem. The final short month is called Pagumen.

The first day of Maskarem, September 11 on the Gregorian calendar (September 12 in leap year), is Enkutatash, or New Year's Day. It coincides with the end of the "big rains" and the greening of the countryside. It is also the feast of Saint John the Baptist. At the churches there are prayers, songs, and processions. In the villages, the children visit their neighbors and relatives with bunches of wildflowers and are given a handful of *dabo* as a treat.

About two weeks later, on September 27, comes the great holy day and public holiday of Maskal. The word *maskal* means "cross," and this day commemorates the finding of the Cross, on which Jesus was crucified, by Saint Helena, the mother of the Roman Emperor Constantine, in the fourth century.

By this time of year the golden Maskal daisies cover the slopes and meadows of the Ethiopian countryside. On the eve of Maskal, in every town and village, a *demera* is built, a tall conical arrangement of wooden poles decorated with golden daisies. The completed *demera* is blessed with incense and a procession of villagers or townspeople, led by the priests and other clergy, circles the *demera* three times. Then, as dusk falls, the *demera* is set aflame to symbolize the flame of burning incense that guided Saint Helena to the exact location of the true cross in Jerusalem.

Many lambs and chickens are slaughtered for the feast, and singing and dancing continue far into the night. On the following day, Maskal, people draw a cross on their foreheads with the charcoal from the dead fires of the previous night, feasting resumes, and the day is spent in visiting and merry-making.

November and December see the celebrations of various saint's days—Saint Michael's on November 22, Saint Mary's on December 1, and Saint Gabriel's on December 28. On these occasions, as on all holy days, work stops, clean *shammas* are donned to attend church services, and the *tabot* is taken from the church and carried in procession, with dancing and singing led by the *dabtaras*.

The Ethiopian Christmas, like that of the Eastern Orthodox Church, falls on January 7. It is called Genna and, while not among the most important of Ethiopia's religious holidays, church services are held, with ceremonial dances accompanied by sounds of sistra and prayer sticks. The sistrum, or *tsenatsel,* is a rattlelike percussion instrument with rows of metal rods set crosswise within a spade- or pear-shaped frame. The rods are strung with small metal discs that make a jingling sound when the sistrum is shaken.

The prayer stick, or *makamiya,* is a long pole with a T-shaped, crutchlike top. It is used to tap the beat of the dance and also serves as an underarm support for the clergy during the lengthy services. A tapering drum with skin stretched over both ends, called a *kabaro,* is another percussion instrument used to accompany religious dances. Melody-producing instruments are not used in religious ceremonies.

Late in the afternoon on Genna day, the hockeylike game known as *genna* is played. Using curved wooden sticks, two teams composed of older boys and young men attempt to drive a wooden or hard leather ball over a goal line. *Genna* is a rough game, the excitement runs high at this once-a-year event, and the playing often continues until darkness falls. The competition may be between villages, with the game played on an open field, or it may be played on a village main street as a local contest.

Small children may receive simple presents from their parents on Genna but Christmas gift giving, as practiced in other parts of the Christian world, is not traditional in Ethiopia.

Timkat, or Epiphany, falls on January 19 and is, along with Maskal, a colorful and uniquely Ethiopian festival. Timkat celebrates the baptism of Christ in the River Jordan. On January 18, the eve of the holy day, the *tabot* is carried from the church in a glorious procession and taken to a nearby lake, stream, or pond of sanctified water. White-turbanned priests, deacons, and *dabtaras,* with prayer sticks, drums, and sistra, hold aloft the intricately designed processional crosses. Brilliant flashes of color are provided by the rich ceremonial robes and by the gorgeous fringed and embroidered umbrellas that are a part of all Ethiopian religious processions. The *tabot* is set down beside the baptismal stream or pond, where it rests throughout the night in a tent guarded by the clergy and by the villagers, who light campfires and eat, drink, sing, and dance until it is time for the early-morning baptismal ceremony. The priests light candles and sprinkle the holy water from the pool or stream on the heads of all those who wish to renew their Christian vows. Some people bathe in the pool, immersing themselves completely in the sanctified water. The procession, bearing the *tabot,* then starts back to the church.

The festivities continue into the next day, January 20, which is a second occasion (in addition to November 22) for celebrating the feast of Saint Michael. Timkat is therefore a three-day holiday that happily blends a deeply religious occasion with a joyous public festival.

Often the exciting national sport of *yeferas guks* is played at Timkat. *Guks* is an exhibition of wildly brilliant horsemanship played on a large meadow by teams of warriors clad in white and wearing lion-mane capes and headdresses. The warriors, on gorgeously decked steeds, wield bamboo lances and are armed with shields of hippopotamus or other tough animal hide. The play consists of pursuit of one horseman by another and the throwing of the lance. *Guks* derives from the mounted-warrior battles of former days, when sharp-tipped javelins were used against the foe, no armor was worn, and the speed and skill of one's horsemanship were the only protection against injury or death. When *guks* is performed nowadays it is usually at Timkat, Maskal, or on some special state occasion.

Easter, or Fasika, is the last of the major feast days of the Ethiopian year and takes place about two weeks later than the Roman Catholic and Protestant Easter of the West.

Fasika is preceded by the eight-week Lenten fast, and the

clergy, along with their devout parishioners, practice total abstinence from food for the last forty-eight hours, beginning with Good Friday. By early Saturday evening the churches are thronged. The special Easter service begins at midnight and ends at dawn on Sunday with the lighting of the Resurrection candles. Ethiopians do not consider that the new day begins at one stroke past midnight, but rather at daybreak. In Addis Ababa, a twenty-one gun salute announces the dawn of Easter Day.

Feasting begins with an early-morning breakfast after church and continues throughout the day, into Easter Monday, and even longer, with sheep slaughtered and many special *wats* prepared for the occasion.

Easter Sunday is rather quietly spent. Many families read from the Bible on this day and play such games as *gebeta,* a chesslike game in which stones or large beans are moved about on a wooden board with sunken cups.

Although Christianity is the official state religion, Ethiopia does have a Moslem and a Jewish population as well. The Falashas, or black Jews, are a small but very unusual religious group, living in villages mainly in the region north of Lake Tana, in Begemder Province. No census has ever been taken of the Falashas, who have been described as the descendents of a lost tribe of Israel, but the Ethiopian government estimates that there are between 60,000 and 70,000 Falashas in Ethiopia.

The Falashas believe that their forebears were Hebrews who, as they were being led out of Egypt and into Palestine by Moses in the thirteenth century B.C., splintered off from their brethren and journeyed south into Ethiopia instead. Historians, however, say that the Falashas are a very old

Hamitic-Semitic people of Ethiopia, whose religion reached them through immigrating Hebrew tribes from southern Arabia, probably well before the Christian era.

For two thousand years or more, the Falashas have been isolated from the mainstream of Judaism. Their knowledge of their religion is based on the Pentateuch, the first five books of the Old Testament, and they are unfamiliar with the later

Falasha mother and child

A Falasha synogogue, crowned with a Star of David

commentaries and interpretations of Hebrew law. They have firmly resisted Christianity and cling to ancient Hebrew traditions such as the baking of matzoth, or unleavened bread, at Passover. Like the Ethiopian Christians and the Moslems, the Falashas do not eat pork, but they do not observe all of the dietary laws of the Hebrew religion.

Through the centuries the Falashas have not known the Hebrew language. Their religious language is the ancient Ghe'ez of the Ethiopian Monophysite Church, and their spoken language is Amharic. In recent years, however, they have begun to learn some Hebrew.

On the surface, the Falasha village with its clusters of *tukuls,* its women grinding *teff* by hand on rough stone "saddles," its farmers, weavers, and blacksmiths, appears no different from the Christian villages. Inside the one-room schoolhouse, however, the children are taught by a rabbi-schoolmaster wearing a skullcap. The synagogue stands on a small rise just beyond the center of the village. It is a round *tukul,* with walls of peeled-sapling posts plastered with clayey mud and with a cone-shaped roof of thatch. An open porch surrounds the building. It appears identical to the Ethiopian Christian country churches of the central highlands except that the peak of the roof is topped with a six-pointed Star of David instead of the usual eight-armed Coptic cross.

A mezuzah, a parchment scroll of writing from the Old Testament rolled up in a tiny case, is affixed to the doorpost of the synagogue, in keeping with Judaic tradition. Inside the circular, mud-plastered prayer room stands a draped wooden chest containing the Hebrew Ark of the Covenant. The ancient Hebrew prayer rituals are strictly observed and Hebrew customs, such as the circumcision of boys eight days after birth, are practiced.

Ethiopian Christians also follow this circumcision custom, further attesting to the similar ancient origins of Judaism and Ethiopian Christianity.

In addition to being farmers, the Falasha are blacksmiths and weavers while the women are potters. Their black pottery figurines, molded by hand out of local clay, are popular decorative objects in many parts of Ethiopia. A favorite Falasha theme is the Lion of Judah with a Star of David perched atop its head.

Ethiopia's Moslems make up slightly more than one-third of the country's total population. In relation to their numbers, Moslems do not play a very important role in Ethiopia's culture or in its social or political life. Moslems were prohibited from owning land in Ethiopia in the past, so many became shopkeepers, traders, and artisans. The main concentrations of the followers of Islam are found on the fringes of the Empire, except for the southwest, which is populated by Negro peoples who follow tribal religions. These comprise Ethiopia's third largest religious group.

The Ethiopian city that has the largest Moslem population is Harar, in eastern Ethiopia, which is believed to have been settled between the seventh and ninth centuries by Moslems from Southern Arabia. The old city of Harar, with its steep cobbled streets, its jumbled shops and dwellings, its *megallah,*

The *megallah,* or Moslem marketplace, at Harar

or Moslem marketplace, and its many mosques, is an Islamic center for Ethiopia.

The chief mosque of old Harar is the whitewashed, twin-minareted Jami Mosque, which was built in the sixteenth century. It was from Harar, in that same period, that Ahmed Gran launched his holy war against the Christians of the highlands. Around 1550, shortly after the death of Gran, the Moslems attempted to fortify their stronghold city by building a five-gated wall around it. The wall stands to this day.

Many predominantly Christian cities have mosques at which the local Moslem population worships. The Moslem

Courtyard of the Jami Mosque in Harar, where Moslems follow the Islamic rule of washing before entering to pray

crier, the muezzin, ascends to the top of the minaret, or prayer tower, five times a day to call the faithful to prayer. The other rituals and beliefs of Islam are also observed.

Despite the Christian-Moslem conflicts of the past and the occasional present-day clashes, complete freedom of religion is guaranteed in Ethiopia today. One Moslem request has been denied, however: permission to build a mosque in the Christian holy city of Axum. The Ethiopian Christian point of view is that the Moslems would be equally reluctant to have an Ethiopian Monophysite Church built in the Moslem holy city of Mecca.

Peasant Christian Ethiopians, particularly those of the older generation, are generally loyal to the church. They make yearly contributions of grain or other produce, goods or money, to their local church, and are sometimes generous beyond their means to priests and *dabtaras*. They try to observe the fasts, attend church services regularly, and do a certain amount of religious reading and praying at home.

The attitudes of young people, however, particularly those who have been educated in government schools, are often at variance with those of their parents. They find the rituals and requirements of the church stiff and old-fashioned. Some prefer to follow Christianity in their own way and disregard the outward forms of their religion. A few students and educated elite of Ethiopia have found a foreign religion, such as one of the branches of Protestantism, to be more compatible with contemporary living. Usually these religions have been introduced through mission schools.

Many young people regard the church as the major stumbling block to progress in Ethiopia. The church schools in turn look with disapproval on those peasant parents who send their children to government schools. Charges that the church impedes improvements in public health and in other areas are not unfounded. Health officers, for example, have reported that peasants often prefer the magic spells and herbal remedies of the *dabtara* to the penicillin, vaccines, and sanitation rules of modern medicine.

Youth groups seeking internal reform have not been especially successful in their attempts to modernize the Ethiopian church. Some churches in the larger cities now permit men and women to sit together during the service. But Ethiopian Christianity traditionally relegates women to a position inferior to that of men, and such superficial changes have little real meaning.

Like the peasantry itself, the church is firmly entrenched in the highlands of Christian Ethiopia. Its authority may be challenged or even disregarded by Ethiopia's emancipated younger people, but this group is still relatively small, and most Ethiopian Christians are a long way from rejecting the 1500-year-old institution that is so dominant in their history and so inherent in their culture.

V

EDUCATION PAST AND PRESENT

Until about 1945 the average Ethiopian child, if he attended school at all, was a student at the local or village church school. His teacher was a priest or *dabtara.* His classroom was a dim mud-walled hut, the shade beneath a small grove of trees, or perhaps some sheltered outdoor spot amidst a jumble of large rocks and boulders.

The subjects he studied were selections from the Old and New Testaments in Ghe'ez and possibly the rudiments of reading and writing Amharic, Tigrinya, or some other local tongue. His textbooks were the parchment scrolls or old manuscripts belonging to the local church, hand-written in Ghe'ez, recording texts from the Bible or possibly church liturgy, hymns, and poetry.

If he was lucky, the church-school student might also have available to him some scrolls or manuscripts, telling the legend of Solomon and Sheba, the lives of the saints, or the chronicles of the Ethiopian kings and the victories of their armies.

All teaching was by memory drill and, except for those

students who were planning a life's work as a priest or *dabtara,* there seemed little point in continuing the narrow and dreary studies beyond the first few years. Girls did not attend the church schools, as education for women was considered unnecessary.

The sons of the Ethiopian nobility and of the wealthy did receive some secular education, mainly at the foreign schools that were established in Addis Ababa in the early 1900's. The first Ethiopian public, or "government," school was opened in 1908 in Addis Ababa by Emperor Menelik II and was attended mainly by the sons of the elite. In order to continue their education, these fortunate few were sent abroad to study.

An enormous gap existed between the Ethiopian university graduate with the foreign diploma and the semi-ignorant church-school student, whose textbooks had consisted of a few aged religious scrolls.

When His Imperial Majesty Haile Selassie I returned to Ethiopia in 1941, after the end of the Italian occupation, he began to make plans for a modern public-school system. Schoolhouses and teaching equipment were almost nonexistent, but by far the most serious problem was the lack of teachers.

Soon, foreign teachers, including many from India, were invited to staff Ethiopia's new public schools. The salaries paid were too low for most European teachers, and the living conditions in the villages and even in the towns were crude for most Westerners.

The new government-run school system featured the introduction of English as a second language. Although the Emperor himself had attended a French mission school in his boyhood, his years of exile in England during the Italian

Gatehouse, part of the Church of Debre Berhan Selassie at Gondar, where school classes are held on the balcony level

occupation and the strong role played by Britain in the liberation of Ethiopia, had given added cultural and political importance to this foreign language. Also, as a result of the years of British rule in India, English was the second language of the Indian instructors who came to Ethiopia to teach.

The church, of course, disapproved of Ethiopian Christians

sending their children to nonreligious schools where they would be influenced by foreign and non-Christian teachers. Despite all these obstacles, the Ethiopian government did manage to put 20,000 Ethiopian children into public schools by 1945.

This figure increased dramatically in the next twenty-five years. By 1971, there were well over half a million students enrolled in schools in Ethiopia. The majority of them were enrolled in government-run schools, although this figure includes students in private, mission, and church schools as well. It covers primary grades (6 years), junior secondary grades (2 years), senior secondary schools (4 years), technical-vocational secondary and higher schools (with courses of varying duration), and the university.

The twenty or thirty government primary schools that existed in 1945 had grown to over a thousand by 1971. There had been virtually no public schools beyond the primary level in 1945 and, of course, no university.

By 1971, however, there were over 200 junior secondary public schools, about 50 senior secondary public schools, more than 50 technical and vocational public schools, and there was Haile Selassie I University with its eleven colleges and faculties. Most important, there were four public Teacher Training Institutes in 1971, located in the key cities of Addis Ababa, Asmara, Harar, and Debre Berhan. As a result, nearly 10,000 Ethiopians were teaching in the primary schools and over 2000 in the secondary schools. Adult education was also being stressed, following the initiation of a national literacy campaign in 1963.

However, despite these striking increases in the number of schools, students, and native-born teachers, education in Ethiopia still has a long way to go. Only 12 percent of all the primary-school-age children in Ethiopia are enrolled in schools of any kind—and 90 percent of Ethiopia's population is still illiterate.

Of Ethiopia's more than one thousand public elementary schools, about 150 are located in Addis Ababa, which has a population of 700,000. This means that the percentage of children who attend primary school in Addis Ababa is much larger than the percentage for the country as a whole.

The W. Zerfeshiwal School (named for Woizero Zerfeshiwal, a relative of Emperor Haile Selassie) is a typical Ethiopian primary school, including grades one through six. It is located in Addis Ababa, on the immediate outskirts of the sprawling main section of the capital. The school has 1300 students, about 600 girls and 700 boys. The proportion of girls to boys drops sharply in Ethiopian schools after the primary-school years.

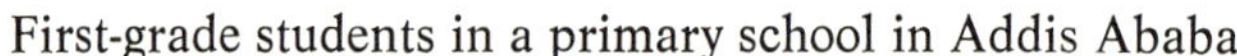

First-grade students in a primary school in Addis Ababa

The school has thirty-two teachers, not really enough, especially as some of them are specialists who teach only gardening, home economics, or crafts, so most classes are crowded, with fifty or fifty-five students to a teacher. The principal of the school is a woman, an Addis Ababa-born Ethiopian who received her teacher-training in India. It is unusual for a woman to hold such a position.

The W. Zerfeshiwal School was built in the Ethiopian year 1958, or the Gregorian-calendar year 1965. It is a single-story, horseshoe-shaped building of gray boards and corrugated-tin roofing. Its classrooms, which are strung out along the two arms of the structure, are small and cramped. The "hand-work" room where six- and seven-year-old girls sit doing sewing, knitting, crocheting, or whatever busywork they please, is dim and crowded. These young children feel at ease here, for this schoolroom resembles the rooms in the one- or two-room tin-roofed homes from which most of them come.

Older primary-school girls having a singing lesson

Most Ethiopian public-school buildings are not examples of sleek modernity, and many of the children attending them may come to school barefoot and in patched clothing. But the spirit of the teachers and administrators and the eagerness for learning on the part of the students are very promising factors.

Also, parents take pride in sending their children to school and some even give their youngsters a little preschool training in reading and writing Amharic. Beginning English is usually taught in the third grade, but at the W. Zerfeshiwal School, the principal sees to it that the children begin learning a little oral English in grade one.

Children must be six years old in order to enter primary school, but most first-graders say they are seven, as this seems the safer figure. Even three- and four-year-old Ethiopian youngsters, when asked their age, often glance up hopefully and report that they are seven, a good school-qualifying age.

School life in Ethiopia, like home life, is largely lived outdoors. A number of school hours are spent on the playing fields that surround the W. Zerfeshiwal School or at a music or singing lesson held beneath a clump of trees. A favorite subject with boys is farming practice in the vegetable gardens laid out in front of the school building.

As all of the children at the W. Zerfeshiwal School live in the surrounding neighborhood, they walk to school and go home for lunch. School hours are from 8:45 to 11:45 and continue from 2:15 to 4:15. There are extracurricular activities from 4:15 to 5:00.

The teaching staff at the W. Zerfeshiwal School is recruited from Ethiopia's Teacher Training Institutes. Since most graduates of these institutions at the present time are men, the school has a majority of male teachers. The few

Boys in primary school at farming practice in the school vegetable garden

women teachers are given assignments in the beginning grades. The starting salary for a primary schoolteacher is $250 Ethiopian per month. As the Ethiopian dollar is equal to forty cents in United States money, this salary works out to $100 U.S. per month.

The school year, as in most parts of Ethiopia, runs from just after Maskal, or the end of September, to the end of June. The annual school vacation lasts for about three months, running through the rainy months of July, August, and September. Schools close for about fifteen days in January for Genna and Timkat and for about ten days at Fasika.

Ethiopian students who are serious about obtaining an education complete their six years of primary school and go on to the two-year course in the junior secondary school and the four-year course in the senior secondary school. Here the struggle to succeed academically takes place in earnest, for the graduate of the senior secondary school must obtain an Ethiopian School Leaving Certificate if he wants to go on to the university or if he wants to get a relatively good job after high-school graduation.

Cramming for the twelfth-grade exams that yield the E.S.L.C. is intensive. Students who fail to obtain the certificate have to make their own way, looking for some institution of higher education that will take them or for a job that recognizes and rewards their years of schooling. Having come this far in their education, students who fail the E.S.L.C. exams find it difficult to rejoin the world of the minimally educated and are often humiliated by the menial and low-paying jobs that they are offered.

There are, of course, many secondary-level technical, commercial, agricultural, and other types of vocational schools

A group of Gondar senior secondary-school students strolling home

in Ethiopia. Boys often select courses in the automotive, aeronautical, or electrical trades, in radio and communications; girls may want to study homemaking, child care, needlecrafts, or typing or other business courses. Traditional attitudes toward the roles of the sexes are still very strong, even among the more enlightened Ethiopians.

The main educational goal for advanced students is Haile Selassie I University, which was founded in 1951 under the name of The University College of Addis Ababa. Ten years later, in 1961, a complex of several colleges and faculties had developed around this nucleus and the entire institution was renamed Haile Selassie I University.

In 1971, Haile Selassie I University celebrated the twentieth anniversary of its founding. Its eleven colleges and faculties include the Addis Ababa-based Arts and Science

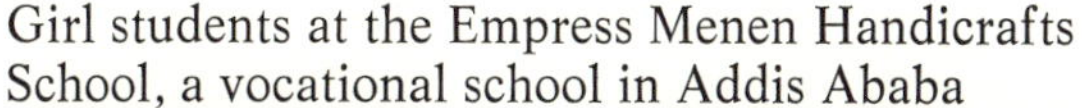

Girl students at the Empress Menen Handicrafts School, a vocational school in Addis Ababa

Faculties, the Faculty of Technology, Faculty of Education, Theological College, College of Business Administration, Faculty of Law, School of Social Work, and Faculty of Medicine, as well as the Public Health College at Gondar and the College of Agriculture at Alemaya, near Harar.

The Public Health College at Gondar, which was established in 1953, is the largest institution of its kind in Ethiopia. It trains health officers, community nurses, and sanitarians for the government's all-important health program. Prior to the 1950's, almost no public-health services were available in Ethiopia. Even at the present time, it is estimated that modern health services are available to only about one-quarter of the population. There are now about 84 hospitals, 64 health centers, and fewer than 400 licensed physicans in Ethiopia. The Faculty of Medicine at the university has so far graduated ten doctors. The rest are either foreigners or Ethiopians who have taken their medical degrees abroad. The university's medical school hopes soon to be graduating thirty doctors a year.

Until 1968 the preferred areas of study at Haile Selassie I University were the arts, business, and agriculture. At present the largest percentage of graduates is from the Faculty of Education, which is the largest single unit in the university. Most of these well-trained teachers join the staffs of Ethiopia's senior secondary schools. In this way the university feeds itself more and better-qualified students each year.

Doctors, teachers, health and welfare personnel, and agricultural extension workers are all badly needed in Ethiopia, for professional-training institutions got off to a late start. Yet progress in the past twenty years has been good.

When The University College of Addis Ababa was founded in 1951, it had 70 students and 4 instructors. In 1971, there were 4500 regular students, 2500 extension students, and over 500 academic staff members at Haile Seleassie I University. The number of girl students increased from about 35 in 1961 to 365 in 1971—still a considerable minority.

The teaching staff at the university is now over 40 percent Ethiopian; most other instructors are American and British. All instruction at the university is in English. Degrees offered at present are on the baccalaureate level, with the exception of the medical degree.

Education is free in Ethiopia on all levels including the university. Students who must live away from home in order to attend the university receive a government stipend of $50 Ethiopian per month to cover their lodging, their food, and some incidental expenses. Strict budgeting is required. Books may be taken on loan from the college bookstore for a nominal deposit.

The drop-out rate is high at the university. Many students suffer financial or academic difficulties, but the young-adult student is also often subjected to family and social pressures, for Ethiopian society as a whole still finds the idea of higher education unfamiliar and baffling. Some students are made to feel ashamed of the fact that in their late teens and early twenties they are not fulfilling the traditional role as providers, husbands, and even fathers. For every six students that enter the university, only one graduates.

An interesting aspect of the study program at Haile Selassie I University is the field service that many students perform, generally in the third year of their college course. Known as Ethiopian University Service, this program was begun in 1965. Its aim was to establish relevance between learning and practice by having each student go on a nine-month field mission connected with his course of study. An

An engineering student in the Faculty of Technology at Haile Selassie I University

engineering student might assist in the building of a road or bridge. An agricultural student might advise resettled farmers about a new planting program, public-health students might work in a village health center, a law student might give a series of law lectures to military and police officers in a provincial capital. Many education students spend their field-service year teaching school and giving adult literacy courses.

Students in the Arts Faculty at Haile Selassie I University at work on a copy of the city's famed Lion of Judah statue

Contacts between university students and Ethiopians from remote or unfamiliar parts of the country are a first step in developing new awarenesses for both. The engineering student whose home is in Asmara in the north, Ethiopia's second largest city, may find himself engaged in road-building among the Nilotic peoples of the southwest. Often such students encounter language differences, strange foods, and unusually crude lodging conditions. These, too, are learning experiences. A stipend of $175 Ethiopian per month is given each student for living expenses during his nine months of national field service.

Once he has earned his degree, diploma, or certificate at Haile Selassie I University, the Ethiopian student looks longingly toward the prospect of taking graduate work or a higher degree at some university abroad, preferably in Europe, the United States, or Canada. Only a small number achieve this goal, but even without travel abroad the educated Ethiopian has been exposed to an international world through his years at the university.

Not only does the university-educated person develop new and wider views of the world, but he begins to see his own country, its conditions and its problems, in a new light. The total number of degree-holding university graduates in Ethiopia is still small—numbering only in the thousands at the present time. Yet there can be little doubt that they form a powerful elite and are destined to be the opinion makers, the movers and doers, and probably the major political influences in the Ethiopia of the future.

VI
JOBS AND THE ECONOMY

THE ETHIOPIAN PEASANT-FARMER, WITH HIS FAMILY-sized fields of grain and his small herd of livestock, makes up the broad base of the Ethiopian economy.

In fact, ninety percent of Ethiopia's population is engaged in agriculture, most of it small-scale, with peasant families planting and reaping just enough food for their own subsistence. At the present time, only about fifteen percent of Ethiopia's total farm product ever gets to market. And, of this portion, much is bartered for other basic items rather than sold for cash.

Ethiopia's agriculture remains primitive chiefly because of the economic and social traditions of rural people. These, in turn, are rooted in the ruggedness of most of Ethiopia's terrain and the fact that it has remained almost completely undeveloped for surface transport through the centuries. Even in the 1970's, it is estimated that nearly eighty percent of Ethiopia's villages and rural homesteads have no access road to the world outside their immediate vicinity. Contacts are limited to those communities that can be reached on foot or by mule in the space of one or two days' travel. Isolation has been a way of life for thousands of years in most of the nearly five million farm households that dot the Ethiopian countryside.

There are other problems, too. Even if the average farmer decided to produce much more food than his family required, he would have many difficulties in addition to transporting it to a major market. He would be unable to get a loan to help him pay for the extra seed, the more sophisticated farm equipment he would need, or the additional labor he would have to take on, for there is no agricultural credit system yet operating in Ethiopia. Once he got his crop to market he would be at the mercy of a highly uncertain cash return, for there is no price structure or subsidy arrangement for farm products in Ethiopia. Even the basic step of obtaining advice on how to improve the yield from his croplands would be a problem. At present, Ethiopia has only about 120 agricultural extension stations to serve its millions of farm households.

A small village market

The pattern of land ownership in Ethiopia also limits the development of farming beyond the family-subsistence level. About one-third of the land is owned by the church, one-third by the government and the royal family, and one-third by private landlords, including large and small landowners, tribal groups, and a very few foreign investors. Much privately owned land is held under various tenancy arrangements, with the land tenant paying the landowner in a share of the crop. And in almost all cases Ethiopian farm units are small. Many are fifteen or twenty acres; often there are five acres or less to a family. This is another reason why farming yields in Ethiopia are not likely to increase.

Social and religious customs, too, have prevented drastic changes in the pattern of Ethiopian farming, just as they have in the overall pattern of Ethiopian rural life. Even though some young people are beginning to seek other livelihoods and life styles, enough still cling to agriculture, which is considered a manly and honored calling, to keep the farming population stable.

Then, too, Ethiopians traditionally eat a limited diet of staples that keep for a long time. There is little or no local demand for leafy greens or other perishable vegetables or for fruits. So, a few basic crops, with a single yearly harvest of each, are sufficient for the average farm family. Cereal grains such as *teff* (from millet), durra (from grain sorghum), barley, corn, and wheat are grown on about seventy-five percent of Ethiopia's cultivated cropland. Most of these crops are for human consumption, as animals traditionally graze for their food.

Next in importance to grains are the legumes—chick peas, lentils, field peas, and various kinds of beans, all of which can be dried for use throughout the year. Oil-bearing seeds (linseed, sesame, sunflower, groundnut, castor bean, cottonseed, and others), honey, coffee, *berberi* peppers, and other spices, all grown or traded in the farming locality, supply the makings for year-round family meals, along with occasional meat or poultry from the family's livestock.

Religious tradition also keeps small-scale farming stable, for it dictates Ethiopian dietary patterns for the numerous religious fast days. As a result, Ethiopian Christians tend to maintain a low yearly per capita intake of food. (It is rare to see an Ethiopian Christian peasant-farmer with any extra flesh on his bones.) The church allows no field work on holy days and gives approval to the farmer who spends as much time as he can at church or at prayers and religious contemplation at home. All in all, the Ethiopian peasant-farmer has little incentive to produce more food than he and his family actually need.

Starvation, on the other hand, is not an immediate threat in Ethiopia, except in the event of a drought year. The Empire has a low population density, only about fifty-three persons per square mile, and two-thirds—possibly as much as sixty-eight percent—of Ethiopia's total acreage is suitable for cultivation. At present, only eleven to fourteen percent of this land is being used for farming. Climate, too, is favorable, and with irrigation and improved farming methods several varied and profitable crops a year could be produced for both domestic and foreign consumption. Despite present trends, these factors favor vastly increased agricultural production for Ethiopia at some time in the future.

There are only a few large-scale agricultural enterprises in Ethiopia, and most of these were established through foreign investment.

On the Wonji Sugar Plantation, where the cane is both grown and processed

Until after the establishment of the Dutch-Ethiopian sugarcane industry in 1950, all of Ethiopia's sugar had to be imported. Ethiopian-grown sugar, most of which is produced on three large plantation estates, is now sufficient to meet nearly all domestic needs, and some is even being exported.

The Wonji Sugar Plantation is located southeast of Addis Ababa in the valley of the Awash River, which is used to irrigate the cane fields. The plantation is an outstanding example of a modern agricultural and industrial operation. The sugar is both grown and processed on the estate.

Both the management, consisting of Dutch and Ethiopian personnel, and the workers, all of whom are Ethiopian, live on the estate. The roomy workers' cottages, set out in neat rows, are the envy of many Ethiopians. The plantation has its own schools, stores, hospitals, and labor relations and welfare offices. Such planned communities are rare in Ethiopia.

Some of the country's cotton crop is grown on large plantations under foreign concession. Tropical and semitropical fruits are commercially grown, mainly for export, in some parts of Ethiopia. In Eritrea Province especially, fruit orchards and vineyards have been developed by Italian growers. Tangerines, tomatoes, and papayas are also grown there, and shipments of such produce are loaded daily at Asmara onto Ethiopian Airlines' flights bound for Rome.

Ethiopia's major export crop, by far, is coffee. This mainstay of the Ethiopian economy accounts for fifty to sixty percent of the total value of all Ethiopia's exports.

The coffee plant grows wild in Ethiopia, particularly in the southwest. It is believed that coffee takes its name from Kaffa Province, where there are dense coffee forests and growth is extensive. Jimma, capital city of Kaffa Province, is an important center for the coffee trade. Coffee is also grown in Hararge Province, in eastern Ethiopia, but most of the Hararge crop is produced on large plantations of cultivated coffee plants.

The United States imports up to seventy-five percent of Ethiopia's total coffee export. The coffee is purchased in the bean and is processed and blended in the United States. Ethiopia expects to set up a processing plant for freeze-drying some of its coffee crop in the near future. Being able to sell coffee in processed form would, of course, bring in higher revenues, provide employment for Ethiopian workers, and would mean a step toward new industrial development.

* * *

Ethiopia's enormous livestock population has great economic potential. Hides, skins, meat, and dairy products could someday equal or surpass coffee as exports in strong demand on the world market.

At present, however, livestock and livestock products, although second in value to coffee, make up only about one-eighth of the total value of Ethiopian exports. The major reasons are poor breeding and feeding practices and long journeys to market, resulting in low milk and poor-quality meat yields. The dairy potential of Ethiopia's cattle is, in fact, so poorly realized that Ethiopia actually imports much of its butter from neighboring Kenya.

Parasitic infections and death from contagious diseases are serious problems for cattle herds. Although most herds kept for subsistence farming are small, numbering about twenty head, cattle are often accumulated beyond the proper market age. It is, of course, considered a sign of wealth and prestige among peasants and nomads to have a large herd of cattle or other livestock.

It is estimated that Ethiopia's peasant-farmers, nomads, and small herders—large-scale ranches are few or nonexistent—possess a total of over fifty million head of livestock. About twenty-five million are cattle, or one to every person in Ethiopia's population.

The rest are sheep and goats, with a slightly larger proportion of sheep. There are about one million camels in Ethiopia, used as a source of meat and milk and as pack animals in the arid lowlands. Swine are kept in very small numbers, about 10,000 to 15,000, due to the Christian and Moslem taboos against eating pork. Hogs are raised mainly for the foreign populations of the larger cities.

Nearly all Ethiopian cattle are of the zebu, or humpbacked, variety. The humps over the animals' shoulders are really fatty areas in which a reserve of nourishment can be stored against the dry season when grazing is poor. By the end of the long dry season in the highlands, their humps are markedly reduced and their flanks are so withered that they have been described as "walking xylophones." Fat-tailed sheep are also common in Ethiopia, for this variety adapts in the same way to long spells of poor feeding.

Crafts such as weaving, pottery, leatherworking, and metalworking have always been essential to Ethiopia's prim-

A village weaver

itive economy. Yet, strangely enough, many rural peoples do not practice these crafts and even look down upon those who do.

The Amharas and the Tigreans consider farming and herding to be highly acceptable occupations, but traditionally they hold the manual arts in low esteem. There is a strong superstition among many Amhara, Galla, and Somali people concerning ironworkers. They believe that all blacksmiths are sorcerers, possessed of the devil, who turn themselves into hyenas at night and feed on the bodies of the dead.

The weaver or blacksmith in many an Amhara village may

A Falasha woman potter producing pottery items for her Amhara neighbors who do not practice this craft

Traditional Ethiopian household stools

be an outcast from some other Amhara village or an Ethiopian from a different tribal or religious group. The Falashas of Ethiopia are blacksmiths, potters, and weavers to many of their Amhara neighbors in Begemder Province. Although their skills are necessary to their fellows, they are sometimes shunned because of them.

Of course, many handcrafted articles are produced in Ethiopia, some for domestic use and some as gifts or souvenirs for the tourist trade. The city of Harar, in the eastern part of the country, has long been a center for the weaving of fine and intricate basketry items such as the *masob*, the round straw table on which Ethiopian meals are served, as well as trays, baskets, bowls, and vases.

The southwest is a center for woodcarving, particularly the low three-legged Jimma stools used in Ethiopian households. Musical instruments and religious materials, especially silver or silver-alloy chest-pendant crosses, priests' crosses, and processional crosses of brass, copper, iron, and wood, are some of the articles made by craft workers.

Nevertheless, the manual arts have not generally enjoyed a high status or wide acceptance in Ethiopia. This situation is sometimes blamed for the slow development of industry in the country and for the scarce supply of workers with high manual-dexterity skills. The idea of working for someone else for a wage or salary has also traditionally been frowned upon by many Ethiopian peoples.

Few Ethiopians have become involved in the operation of small businesses, because trade is considered a low calling. Most shopkeepers, merchants, traders, and proprietors of small workshops in Ethiopia are of foreign origin, usually Arabs, Indians, Greeks, and Armenians. The large number of Yemenite and other small-business operators from the Arabian peninsula is due in part to the existence of laws prohibiting Moslems from owning land in Ethiopia.

One noteworthy enterprise under Ethiopian management is the medium-sized business known as the United Abilities Company. This unique factory-workshop was set up in 1964 in Addis Ababa and recently moved to new enlarged quarters.

The United Abilities Company serves a dual purpose: it is the only umbrella factory in all of Ethiopia, and it is staffed almost completely by blind, deaf, and severely crippled workers, many of whom were previously beggars or totally dependent on their families for economic survival.

Ethiopians buy about 750,000 umbrellas per year. These include ceremonial umbrellas for religious use: large-sized golf, lawn, and garden-table umbrellas; and the numerous sunny-weather and rainy-season umbrellas, both regular and folding types, that Ethiopians traditionally carry whenever they set forth in city streets or on country roads. Yet, until 1964, all Ethiopian umbrellas were imported and had to be paid for in precious foreign currency.

Having started with a workshop of 27 disabled employees, a subsidy from Ethiopian government welfare organizations, and an Ethiopian bank loan, the company now engages 260 workers. The workers assemble about 2500 umbrellas a day, using foreign-made components and imported textiles.

The employees at United Abilities work an eight-hour day and a five-and-a-half-day week, less than the forty-eight-hour maximum established by law. While Ethiopia has no minimum-wage law at the present time, the disabled employees at the United Abilities factory receive salaries that are on a par with those of able-bodied workers in similar types of work:

A Moslem blanket merchant in Addis Ababa's Mercato

about $40 to $60 Ethiopian per month ($16 to $24 U.S. per month). If these salaries seem low compared to those earned by production-line workers in other countries, it must be remembered that the current per capita income for Ethiopia is only $66 U.S. a year.

On the whole, industrial activity in Ethiopia is relatively small, even though it has been growing steadily since the late 1950's. At present there are about 300 major industrial plants in the country. Most are engaged in food processing (sugar, spices, beverages, canned meats), in textile production (yard goods, linens, wool blankets, and carpets), and in the manufacture of building materials (cement, bricks, tin roofing). Paper, shoes, and glassware are also manufactured. Nearly all industrial products are produced for Ethiopia's domestic market. Exports of manufactured products currently are quite limited.

The disabled employees of the United Abilities Company produce nearly all the umbrellas for Ethiopia's large domestic market.

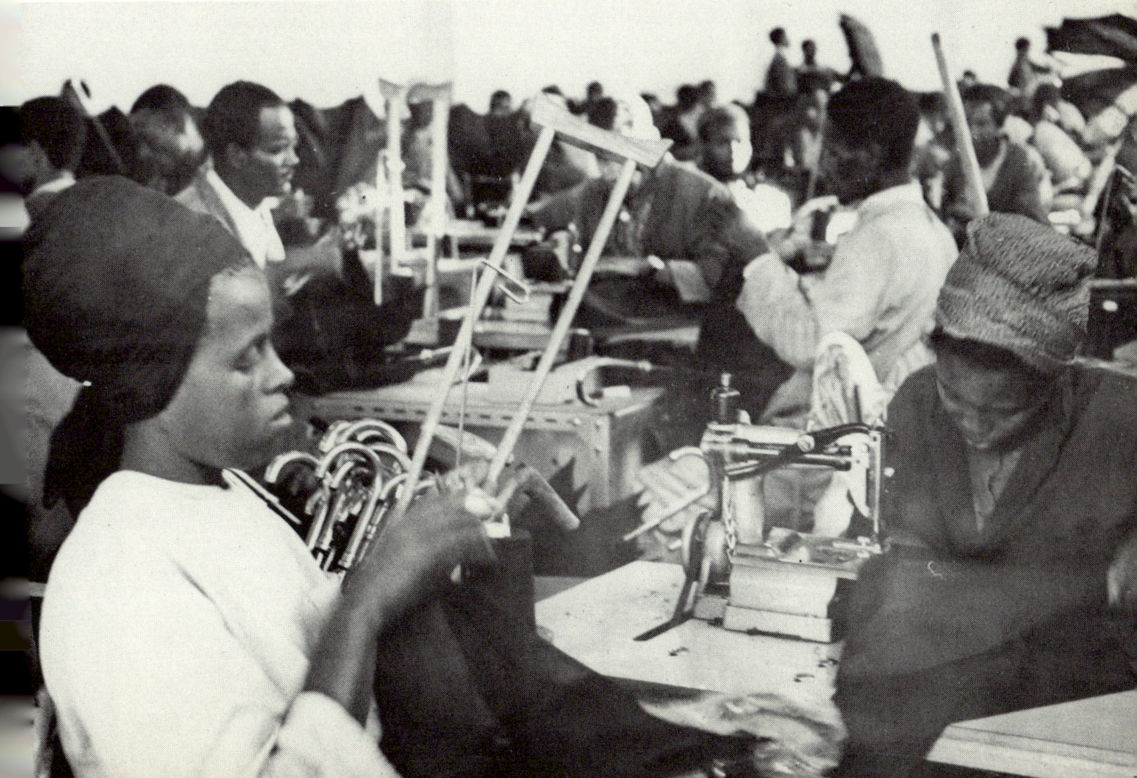

Mining is not extensive in Ethiopia, for the Empire's mineral resources have remained largely unexplored. Ore deposits are believed to lie deep beneath the earth's surface, but both the terrain and the lack of transportation facilities present serious drawbacks to investigators. Some gold is mined in southern Ethiopia; salt is evaporated from sea water at Massawa, and salt is mined in the Danakil Depression, which also has large deposits of potash.

Ethiopia does have adequate hydroelectric power for its industrial, mining, and transportation needs, and for its limited consumer demand. Major power installations are on the Awash River, at Koka Dam, which was built in 1960, and at two other stations on the Awash south of Addis Ababa. There is a hydroelectric power station at the Blue Nile Falls and a few smaller installations around the country.

Lack of adequate freight-transportation facilities in Ethi-

Men about to roof the local church before the onset of the rainy season with tin produced by Ethiopia's building-materials industry

opia remains a problem for industrial development, as it does for mining exploration and agricultural development.

The country has two railway lines. The 486-mile Franco-Ethiopian Railway is jointly owned and operated by the governments of Ethiopia and France. The railroad was begun in 1894 and completed in 1917. It connects Addis Ababa with the French-territory port of Djibouti on the Gulf of Aden. The second railroad is a 191-mile, Italian-built line in Eritrea Province. It was completed in 1922 and connects the port of Massawa with Asmara, continuing a short distance westward to the town of Agordat.

Ethiopia's ocean shipping is from its two Red Sea ports of Massawa and Assab. Goods may also be shipped by sea from the port of Djibouti, located in what was formerly called French Somaliland but is now the French Territory of the Afars and Issas.

Air transportation has proved the most effective for passenger travel and cargo shipment. Since 1946, Ethiopian Airlines has been developing and enlarging its international and domestic flight networks. Today dozens of remote corners of the country with tiny grass-landing-strip airfields can be reached in less than an hour's flying time from Addis Ababa, Asmara, Dire Dawa, and Jimma. Ethiopian Airlines, which also has numerous international flights to European, African, and Asian cities, operates under a management-assistance contract with Trans World Airlines.

Addis Ababa's international jet airport serves as a gateway to the country's capital and largest city. Founded in 1886 and declared the new capital in 1889, Addis Ababa has developed from a collection of hillside villages into a sprawling, modern metropolis of 700,000 people.

Its economic growth and international prestige now attract businessmen and diplomats from every part of the world, for the Empire's commercial life flows from Addis Ababa, and it is the site of more than eighty foreign embassies and consulates. A panoramic view shows the city studded with lofty glass-and-concrete office and government buildings as well as the towering new Addis Ababa Hilton Hotel, all symbols of the capital's flourishing present and ambitious future.

The Addis Ababa maintenance division of Ethiopian Airlines

Yet, alongside these edifices, the tin-roofed shanties of the poor huddle in dusty compounds where goats, sheep, and cattle wander freely. The walled villas of the prosperous stand beside hole-in-the-wall workshops where artisans labor by the light of a single bare bulb. Donkeys and other livestock mingle indifferently with the taxis, trucks, small European cars, and ambassadorial limousines that filter through the narrower streets and cruise the broad new boulevards.

The swimming pool of the new Addis Ababa Hilton Hotel modeled after the twelfth-century rock-cut Church of Saint George, at Lalibela

The increased traffic and modern street lighting have driven one vestige of the African past from Addis Ababa's streets. Until half a dozen years ago, hyenas came slinking down from the hills every evening after dark to devour the city's garbage. Today these "garbagemen of Ethiopia" are fearful of entering the city but can still be spotted nightly, just after sunset, scavenging on its outskirts.

Asmara, capital of Eritrea Province and the Empire's second city, with a population of 200,000, is the only other major metropolis in Ethiopia. Like Addis Ababa, it is a young city, dating from the 1880's, when Italy was beginning to extend its colonial influence in Eritrea. With its Italian cultural influences, its palm trees, sidewalk cafés, and Mediterranean-style villas, Asmara today is a jaunty, modern city that has steadily prospered over the years, benefiting mainly from the agricultural and commercial enterprises of Italian investors.

Until the late 1950's, when the demand for manufactured goods began to increase, the value of Ethiopia's imports barely exceeded that of its exports. At one time during this period the Empire actually enjoyed a favorable balance of trade.

However, since the early 1960's, the proportionate value of Ethiopia's imports has been growing steadily over that of its exports. Ethiopian export products will probably continue to be agricultural items almost exclusively: coffee, hides and skins, oilseeds, legumes, fruits, salt, spices, beeswax, *chat,* live animals, fresh and salted beef, and canned meats. Oilseeds go to Japan, Italy, and countries of the Arabian peninsula; sheepskins to the United Kingdom, Italy, West Germany, and France; legumes to many Asian countries; livestock

Asmara, with its palm-lined sidewalks and
Italian culture, "a corner of Italy in Africa"

mainly to Saudi Arabia; and canned meats to Israel and Italy.

Imports are mostly from the world's more highly industrialized countries such as the United States, West Germany, Italy, Japan, the United Kingdom and the Netherlands. They include ships, railway and motor vehicles, aircraft, light and heavy machinery and parts, electrical equipment, fuels, textiles, chemicals and pharmaceuticals, and numerous other manufactured and industrial products; also raw cotton and some foodstuffs.

The trend toward a growing proportion of imports over exports is expected to continue as Ethiopia expands its industrial sector. To offset this imbalance, the government hopes to increase the range and quantity of its agricultural export commodities. Thus, they would be able to diversify their markets and stabilize the economy further. At present, for example, Ethiopia depends heavily—too heavily say some economists—on the United States to buy most of her coffee crop. The government also hopes to increase the value of the export commodities as much as possible by treating or processing them domestically instead of exporting them in their raw state. Coffee beans exported as freeze-dried coffee, livestock exported as canned meats and processed dairy products, hides exported as manufactured footwear—all of these would operate favorably toward balancing Ethiopia's foreign trade. Some of these export possibilities are within reach, others are very long-range. Agricultural growth will also have to keep pace with the slowly growing urban population at home as Ethiopia develops its commercial and industrial sectors.

At present, however, consumer demand for nearly all products is growing very slowly. Relatively few members of Ethiopia's huge rural population have even entered the money economy as yet. They remain highly self-sufficient. For the peasant-farmer on his highland homestead, the nomadic herder of the arid lowlands, the Nilotic tribal peoples of the southwest bushlands, necessities are few and are adequately supplied either locally or through barter.

VII
ARTS AND COMMUNICATION

THE EXPRESSION "WAX AND GOLD" DOES NOT REFER to these two moderately important products of the Ethiopian economy. It refers instead to a special old form of Ethiopian poetry.

The main characteristic of wax and gold composition is the interweaving of two strands of thought with two separate meanings. The wax expresses an obvious or apparent meaning, that which *seems* to tell what the lines of verse are all about. But buried within the wax lies the gold meaning, the intended meaning, for which one must dig more deeply.

The term "wax and gold" comes from the ancient art of the goldsmith. To cast an object in gold—a goblet for example—the goldsmith first made an exact model out of wax. The wax model was packed all around with clay, which hardened into a mold. The wax was then melted and poured away, and the mold was filled with molten gold, which cooled and hardened to become the real goblet, the object originally intended.

Wax and gold poetry was originally cast into a verse form known as *qené*. Traditionally, *qené* was never written down, so it is difficult to know when this cryptic form of literary expression first began to be practiced in Ethiopia. Some scholars have guessed at the fifteenth century. *Qené* verses, usually running from two to eleven lines, were often fitted to the melodies of church chants and would be sung at the close of the church services.

Originally *qené* was composed in Ghe'ez and continues to be today in Ethiopia's monasteries and religious schools. However, Amharic, the spoken and written language of modern Ethiopia, also has subtlety and richness, and it, too, lends itself well to wax and gold composition. The art is being practiced in Amharic by modern Ethiopian writers.

Apart from its use in traditional *qené* poetry, wax and gold has always been and continues to be a useful means of expressing ideas that might otherwise be unpopular or dangerous. In Ethiopia, the institutions of family, church, and government have always been rigid, and open expressions of opposition have not been tolerated. Censorship is still a fact of life in contemporary Ethiopia. Opponents of the current regime, for example, might find wax and gold a useful tool for venting their dissatisfactions, either in writing or in conversation, and for communicating their ideas to their fellows with relative safety. Or wax and gold might be used for any number of other purposes, such as to convey sentiments of love or to express ridicule of a personal enemy.

As wax and gold compositions have seldom been written down, they may be classified as oral literature. Ethiopia does, however, have a large body of written literature, most of it in Ghe'ez and dating from the fourth century, the early days of Christianity in Ethiopia.

While the original fourth-century manuscripts have been lost during the 1500 years that have elapsed since they were produced, later writings do attest to their existence. These earliest works of the Axumite period were mainly translations of the scriptures and other religious writings taken from the Greek. Monks, some of them Syrians by birth, served as translators of these works and produced them with the help of religious scribes.

The richest period for Ethiopian literature began with the restoration of the Solomonic line in 1270 and ended with the Moslem invasions led by Ahmed Gran, which lasted from 1527 to 1543.

The most important Ethiopian literary work of the 1300's, and possibly of all time in Ghe'ez, was the *Kebra Negast* (Glory of Kings). It combined materials found in Arabic sources and in Ethiopian legend, and it set down the story of Solomon and Sheba, and of their son Menelik I, Ethiopia's first ruler of the Solomonic line. Some scholars believe the *Kebra Negast* was written in order to establish more firmly the legitimacy of the then recently restored Solomonic line. It has served to the present day to confer authority upon rulers of that line.

During the fourteenth and fifteenth centuries the works written in Ghe'ez were mainly religious, although there were also stories of the lives of the Zagwé kings, including the much-revered Lalibela. Other nonreligious literature such as poems, songs, histories, and chronicles of war began to appear at this time.

Although the Moslem forces of Ahmed Gran destroyed many manuscripts during their sixteen-year campaign, much Ghe'ez literature survived because copies had been made and hidden away in such places as the island monasteries of Lake Tana and in remote highland monasteries perched atop sheer-faced cliffs, such as Debre Damo.

After the death of Gran and the end of the Moslem threat, new religious works in Ghe'ez began to appear. Some were aimed at those Christians who had converted to Islam in order to insure their survival during the Moslem ferocities and were, of course, intended to bring such Christians back into the fold. Other defenses of Ethiopian Christianity were inspired by the threat of the Jesuit missionaries from Portugal, who began to arrive after the Portuguese had helped put down Gran and who wanted to convert Ethiopia to Roman Catholicism.

A principal work of the seventeenth century was the *Fetha Negast* (Legislation of Kings), which compiled and translated a body of religious and civil laws that had been used by Egyptian Copts in the thirteenth century. It has served as the pattern for much common, civil, and criminal law in Ethiopia right up to the present time.

Amharic, long the spoken language of Ethiopia, began to be the language of Ethiopian literature in the nineteenth century. The Emperor Theodore II, who reigned from 1855 to 1868, decreed that Amharic should be the official language of the Empire, for he saw this as a means of uniting the country.

In 1892 an Amharic version of *Pilgrim's Progress* appeared in Ethiopia. This was followed by a flowering of creative writing, most of it in the form of allegorical tales that bore a religious message. Biographies of Menelik II and other leading Ethiopians appeared in the early years of the twentieth century. Literary production was, however, stifled during the Italian occupation years of 1936 to 1941.

In the years since 1941, a dozen or so writers have come to the fore with novels, short stories, plays, verse dramas, poetry, biographies, and histories. Also, folktales, which had been handed down orally from generation to generation, have been set down in written form for the first time.

One of Ethiopia's best-selling contemporary novelists is Abiye Gubegna. Born in the mid-1930's, Abiye attended church schools for twelve years and became a master of wax and gold poetry. Possibly because he employs this art in his novels as well, some of Abiye's work has been suspected of carrying revolutionary ideas and been turned back by the censors. Nevertheless, he has continued to write, and his output of published work has grown steadily.

Very little by Ethiopian writers has been translated into English. One novel that is available is *Shinega's Village* by Sahle Sellassie, first published in the United States in 1964.

If the number of contemporary writers in Ethiopia seems small, it must be remembered that several handicaps exist. Traditionally, writing has not been highly esteemed in Ethiopia. Like other forms of manual labor, the work of the scribes who prepared and copied the early religious manuscripts and scrolls was often looked down upon. Also, since almost all of the early literature was concerned with religious themes, there was a certain fear of those who dealt with such an awesome subject.

A second obstacle to literary development is that even at the present time there are no commercial publishing houses in the country. Writers must arrange for the printing, distribution, and sale of their own work. And before they can go ahead with such arrangements, they must submit all material to a government censorship board and receive permission to publish.

Lastly, with only about ten percent of the population literate, Ethiopia's reading public is extremely small.

* * *

The earliest pictorial art to be found in Ethiopia appears to be rock paintings, of uncertain date. They show sticklike human and animal figures. As the cattle portrayed are without humps, these paintings are believed to be well over three thousand years old. The humpbacked zebu cattle were introduced into Ethiopia from Asia along with the Semitic immigrations from the Arabian peninsula, which began in about 1000 B.C.

Like its literature, Ethiopian painting on parchment and canvas dates from about the fourth century A.D. and has been mainly on religious themes. Scenes from the Bible, pictures of saints, angels, and the forces of evil were portrayed on the pages of beautifully decorated and lettered manuscripts prepared from calfskin, goatskin, or sheepskin. Such paintings on parchment as well as paintings on canvas going back to the fourteenth century still survive. The in-

The famous ceiling of angels' faces in the seventeenth-century Church of Debra Berhan Selassie at Gondar

teriors of churches were decorated with religious murals that were painted either directly on the walls and ceilings or were applied to canvas, which was then made to adhere to these surfaces.

Ethiopia's early art was very stylized and, for the most part, has remained so throughout the centuries. It can be termed decorative rather than representative. Saints and other godly figures were drawn full-face; evil figures were drawn in profile. All were portrayed in stiff, conventional poses. Colors, outlines, and backgrounds were sharp, clear, and flat, and there was little attempt to show shading or perspective.

Very few nonreligious themes appeared in Ethiopian painting until the nineteenth century. At that time portrayals of famous rulers, battle scenes, hunting scenes, and historical events became popular. A favorite subject in Ethiopian pic-

Stained-glass mural in Addis Ababa's Africa Hall, the work of famed artist, Afewerk Tekle

torial art is the story of Solomon and Sheba, often told in colorful hand-painted cartoon strips of a dozen or more scenes. Scrolls of such cartoons, sometimes with captions in Amharic beneath each scene, are produced in large numbers in present-day Ethiopia to be sold as souvenirs to tourists.

Western painting, both traditional and modern, has had some influence in Ethiopia. However, several of the country's foremost contemporary artists work in abstract styles that are a blend of Ethiopian traditional art and of their own personal response to the world around them. Three who are internationally known are Skunder Boghossian, Gebre Kristos Desta, and Afewerk Tekle. Afewerk Tekle has done many striking murals in Ethiopian public buildings and is perhaps best known for his rich, jewellike stained-glass window murals in Addis Ababa's Africa Hall.

The development of sculpture in Ethiopia has been limited

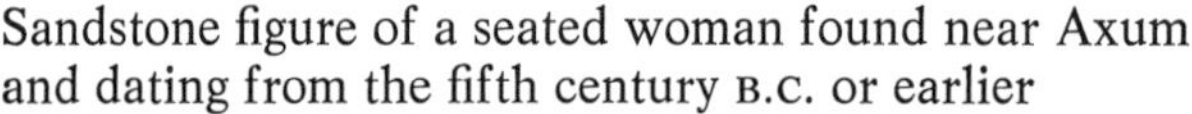

Sandstone figure of a seated woman found near Axum and dating from the fifth century B.C. or earlier

by the fact that the Ethiopian Christian Church, like most other Eastern Christian churches, frowns on the portrayal of three-dimensional human or animal figures as encouragement of idol worship.

While pre-Christian Ethiopia has turned up some fine examples of human and animal figures carved in stone, works carved in the Christian era have been mainly in geometrical design. The Ethiopian genius for decorative carving is seen in such objects as wooden and filed-iron crosses, and in the interior and exterior stonework of the rock-cut churches in Lalibela and scattered through central and northern Ethiopia. Within some of the churches, there are low-relief carvings of the saints. These figures are mainly pictorial, as they project only slightly from the stone and no part of the body is fully detached from the background.

The inventiveness and skill of Ethiopian decorative artists

A necklace of intricate design showing the skill of Ethiopian decorative artists

Falasha pottery objects, although crude, show artistic imagination and whimsical charm.

are seen in a large variety of ornamental and useful objects —necklaces, ear picks, all types of crosses including the eight-armed Coptic crosses that crown the Christian churches, articles of basketry and pottery, warrior's shields of decorated elephant or hippopotamus hide, and other leatherwork.

Musical expression is a vital part of both the folk and the religious traditions. A particular folk song may be played by a shepherd boy on a simple bamboo flute, called a *washint*, it may be hummed by a peasant woman at her household chores or a farmer in his fields, or it may be played, sung, and danced, with everyone participating, at a gathering celebrating a local festival, a wedding, or the birth of a child.

Ethiopia's folk music is as old as its civilization, while its church music can be traced to the Axumite period and the early days of Christianity in Ethiopia. There is the church liturgy itself, which is always chanted rather than spoken, and then there are also songs and hymns that hold an important place in the religious musical repertory.

Religious chanting is performed in three basic styles. There is a slow, somber chant for Lent, funerals, and important fasts; a plain, or middling-style, chant; and a lighter chant with melodic variations that is used for feast days and happy occasions.

Ethiopian music is based on scales that are unfamiliar in the Western world, and often it sounds strange to the ear of the foreigner. While Ethiopian religious music has been written down since the sixth century, folk music has seldom been recorded in any form.

Folk songs fall into several groups. The *zaffran* are the simple songs of everyday joys and sorrows. They tell of farm and household chores and of local events. They are danced by men and women together, accompanied by handclapping and possibly the beating of a small hand-held drum. Verses are improvised and the words and music change and evolve with new situations and the passage of time.

The *fukara* and the *shilela* are warriors' and patriots' songs. In the *fukara,* a single singer struts before his listeners telling of his valor in the face of a lion, a hippopotamus, or a detachment of enemy soldiers. The singer may be accompanied by a *masinko,* a single-stringed instrument that is played with a bow, or by the very popular lyrelike *krar* that is plucked with the fingers or with a pick. After the first *fukara* has been sung, it is usually followed by a succession of others, each warrior trying to outdo those who preceded him with an increasingly rousing recital of his deeds of bravery.

Funeral occasions call forth a special kind of song, the *mousho,* usually composed and sung by women. These lamentations accompanied by soft handclapping tell of the good qualities of the departed. The *leqso* is also a sad song, telling of past misfortunes or of general unhappiness.

Folk music has been transmitted and perpetuated in Ethi-

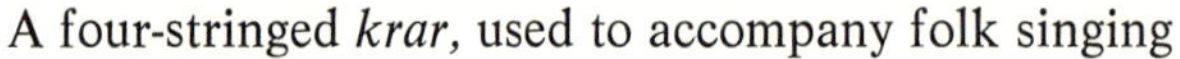

A four-stringed *krar,* used to accompany folk singing

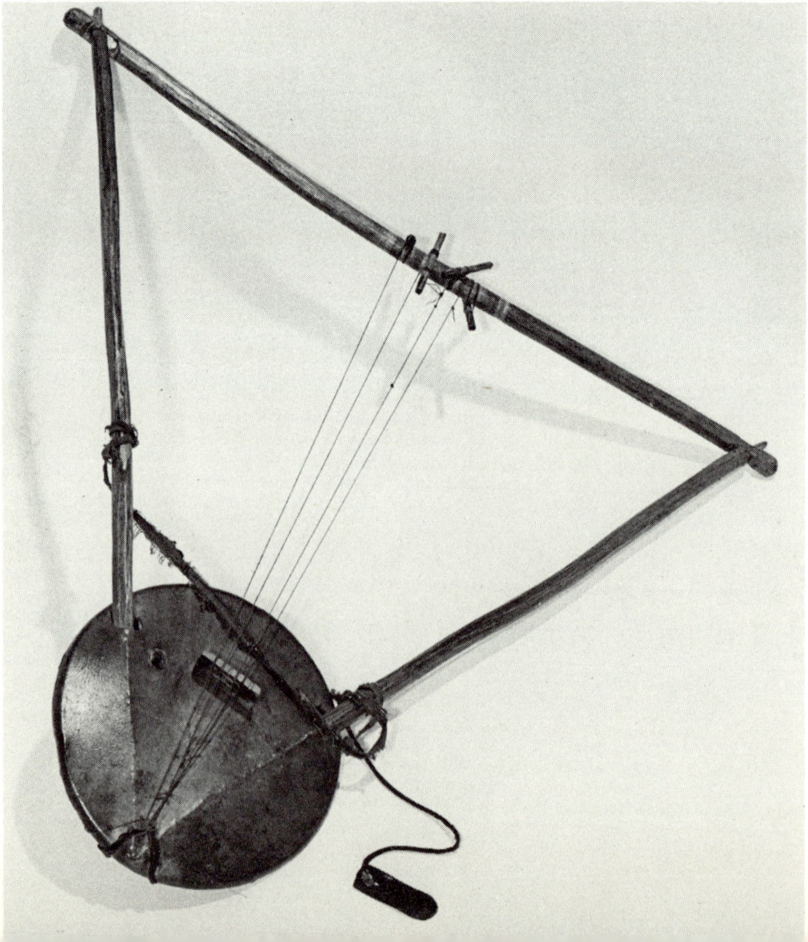

opia largely through groups of wandering minstrels known as *azmari*. The *azmari* can be traced as far back as the twelfth century. They were usually in the employ of the local nobility and were expected to entertain at princely feasts with witty tales and improvised song, accompanied by music performed on the *masinko*. They also performed in the villages and at peasant gatherings. The *azmari* continue to be an important contemporary cultural institution. They have appeared in groups, including both men and women performers, on theater stages and on radio and television.

Less well-known traditional folk singers are the *lalibeloch*, believed to have been organized by King Lalibela. It is thought that the early *lalibeloch* were lepers. It was their custom to sing outside the houses of wealthy and influential people shortly before dawn, their faces completely concealed beneath a *shamma*. This tradition is still carried on today in some parts of Ethiopia. The serenades of the *lalibeloch* are melancholy and moving. When their song is completed, they are usually given money or food and vanish unknown before the day breaks.

Ethiopian folk dances are as varied as the regions and peoples of the Empire and reflect their different backgrounds and temperaments. People of the *kwolla* zones tend to be more vigorous and expressive in their dances, while those of the highlands are graceful and more restrained. However, there are certain similarities throughout. Ethiopian folk dances do not call for intricate steps and fancy footwork. The knees, head, neck, and shoulders are the principal parts of the body involved. Often there is jumping, stomping, handclapping, and swaying from side to side. Facial expressions can be very important to the dance.

The themes for Ethiopian folk dances come from the lives

of the people. For the most part they represent sowing, harvesting, courting, hunting, and episodes of battle.

Today folk dance performances have become a popular form of entertainment in Addis Ababa. The Haile Selassie I Theater, which was established in 1955, has a company of folkloric singers, dancers, and musicians. Along with the National Patriotic Association, an older institution of popular culture that was formed in the early 1930's, the theater group has presented Ethiopian folkloric programs abroad—in the Soviet Union, China, Canada, and Mexico, as well as in many countries closer to home.

Addis Ababa's Haile Selassie I Theater is the national theater of Ethiopia. When it was founded in the twenty-fifth, or Silver Jubilee, year of the reign of Emperor Haile Selassie, it was intended to serve as a showcase for music, drama, and folklore performances.

The presentation of stage plays has been limited to a few original plays in Amharic and some translations of Western plays, ranging from Shakespeare and Molière to the contemporary. The original plans called for the theater to have a drama school and a repertory of twelve plays a year. However, this goal proved too ambitious. At present, the theater produces three plays a year.

The theater has a small orchestra capable of playing some Western music, but visiting opera companies and recitalists must bring their own orchestras or accompanists. Because of performances given there by foreign opera companies, the Haile Selassie I Theater is sometimes called "the Opera" by Addis Ababans. Folklore performances are now the principal live presentations there, and throughout most of the year movies are shown.

Movies are a popular form of entertainment in the larger cities and towns. At present there are only about thirty movie theaters in Ethiopia, of which nine or ten are in Addis Ababa and six in Asmara. All commercial films are imported, most from the United States and the rest from Britain, Italy, and India. Like other media of communication in Ethiopia, all movies must pass the official censorship board, and material that is considered morally or politically dangerous is cut.

Radio broadcasting in Ethiopia began in 1935, but was short-lived due to the Italian invasion and occupation. An important radio event took place on September 13, 1935, when Emperor Haile Selassie made his first appeal to the world for assistance against the Italian Fascist invasion of his country.

The gradual growth of domestic broadcasting after the 1941 liberation resulted in the development of Radio Ethiopia, which today transmits from Addis Ababa, Asmara, and Harar, and reaches about five million listeners, or about one-fifth of the population. The broadcasting schedule includes programs in Amharic, English, Arabic, and local tongues, with programs that range from news, education, and religion to quiz shows, disc jockeys, and women's interests.

Television is still in its infancy, having begun in 1964. Programs are received only in the vicinity of Addis Ababa and reach a very small proportion—probably about one percent—of the population. Programs are in English and Amharic, and schedules extend for five to eight hours a day. Serials and variety shows of American and British origin are shown along with Ethiopian news broadcasts, entertainment features, and educational documentaries.

Both Radio Ethiopia and the Ethiopian Television Service are government-run, under the direct supervision of the Ministry of Information. Commercials are used on radio and television. Radio-set owners do not need a license to tune in on broadcasts, but owners of the 20,000 or so television sets that are located in the private homes, restaurants, and hotels in and around Addis Ababa must pay a license fee of $50 Ethiopian per year for viewing.

Although newspaper publishing began in the early years of the twentieth century in Ethiopia, newspapers and periodicals were crudely produced and very limited in coverage. After the end of the Italian occupation in 1941, newspapers increased in number and quality. Today there are six daily newspapers circulated in Ethiopia, all of which are published in either Addis Ababa or Asmara. There are also several dozen weeklies, monthlies, and quarterlies.

The two most important dailies are the Amharic-language *Addis Zamen* (New Times) and the English-language *Ethiopian Herald,* both published in Addis Ababa. Founded as weeklies in 1941 and 1943 respectively, these newspapers now have circulations of approximately 10,000 and 8000.

Most Ethiopian newspapers and periodicals are government-owned and are subject to regulations of the Penal Code of 1957, which prohibits slander or defamation of the Emperor and other authorities, protects the government and citizens from unwarranted press attacks, outlaws the printing of rumors and reports that might stir racial and religious disturbances, and restricts the publication of certain types of political and military information.

If the censorship of books, newspapers, movies, radio, and television in Ethiopia seems excessively strict, it must be remembered that Ethiopia has had a long history of instability and internal struggle for power. The unification of the Empire only began to come about in the last years of the nineteenth century under Menelik II, and the imperial crown has never sat really securely on any head. How effective such government censorship actually is can be questioned. It should be noted that word-of-mouth communication always has been important in Ethiopia. Traditionally, news and information was spread by the beating of an official drum, followed by the announcements of the royal herald. It is still true today that the vast majority of the people, unable to read and with no access to radio or television, get surprisingly speedy and detailed news reports and information. Such reports reach them verbally from traveling merchants, clergymen, health officials, and others. They are transmitted at such places as weekly markets, village churches, and country crossroads. Rumors, gossip, and undercover stories, too, seem to fly across the stretches of desolate countryside with lightning speed.

VIII
IN THE MAINSTREAM

At the beginning of the nineteenth century Ethiopia was in a state of severe disorder and instability. The power of the imperial court at Gondar had been waning steadily since the mid-1700's. During one period the Galla were in a position of influence in the Gondar government. After that a powerful prince from Tigré took control of the Gondar court, even further weakening the Solomonic line. By 1800 there were half a dozen local dukes and princes vying bitterly for imperial power. The four main contenders were the rulers of the feudal domains of Begemder, Tigré, Gojjam, and Shoa. Today the fourteen provinces of Ethiopia correspond roughly to old feudal divisions such as these.

Civil wars kept Ethiopia in a condition of turmoil until 1855, when a single strong leader finally emerged in the person of Emperor Theodore II. The new emperor was the son of a local chieftain who claimed descent from the Queen of Sheba, but he was not of the direct Solomonic line of the Gondar rulers. Theodore had been born in 1818 and given the name of Kassa. As emperor he took the name Theodore in fulfillment of an old prophecy that a ruler by such a name would lead Ethiopia to glory.

Theodore moved the capital to the fortress site of Magdala, which lay to the southeast of Gondar and was centrally located in the Amhara highlands. Wary and fierce, intent on unifying the Empire as it had never been before, Theodore put down the local princes one after another, systematically breaking up their areas of influence and putting his own loyal people in control as governors. He even made a captive of the crown prince of Shoa, who was later to become Menelik II, and confined him to the fortress at Magdala.

Theodore did not make the mistake of attempting to rule the country from Magdala. He continued to roam the countryside with his armies and his retinue of aides and advisors, just as in the days when he had been a local chieftain moving toward power.

It was during the reign of Emperor Theodore II that a foreign army penetrated the Ethiopian highlands for the first time in the country's history.

As Theodore was recognized to be the principal sovereign of Ethiopia, Queen Victoria of Great Britain had sent a consul to his court in the late 1850's. When a letter that Emperor Theodore had written to Queen Victoria in 1862 went unanswered for two years, Theodore grew enraged and imprisoned the British consul, Captain Charles Duncan Cameron, at Magdala along with a group of other Europeans who were entitled to diplomatic immunity.

It is not certain whether Theodore's letter went unanswered due to a careless slipup in the British Foreign Office or because the British did not wish to commit themselves on Theodore's petition for aid against the Moslems. The Queen's reply to Theodore's letter was finally written in 1864. The letter included a request for the immediate release of the prisoners, but it did not reach Magdala until 1866. Theodore responded by tossing the British envoy who had delivered Victoria's overdue reply in jail as well.

By 1867, the British government had lost patience with Theodore's continued refusal to release the prisoners, and it launched a military campaign under the leadership of Sir Robert Napier. Not an expedition for colonial territory or other gain, the sole purpose of the campaign was to free the Europeans imprisoned atop the fortress-mountain of Magdala, four hundred miles inland from the Red Sea coast.

The British force included soldiers from India and the Near East, numerous camels and mules to carry general supplies, and a contingent of forty-four trained Indian elephants on which were mounted the British cannon. For three months the British expedition inched its way from the narrow coastal plain up through the trackless mountains, building roads as it went and throwing bridges across the gorges. Probably the most amazing sight of all to the incredulous Ethiopian farmers and herdsmen who witnessed the passing expedition were the Indian elephants, tame as oxen, serving as beasts of burden. In Africa, the elephant is a wild species that is almost impossible to domesticate.

When the armies of Emperor Theodore and Lord Napier finally confronted one another near Magdala in April of 1868, the battle was swift and decisive. Theodore's one big gun, made for him by a group of European artisans, exploded its charge and promptly burst into fragments. The triumphant British received the released prisoners while the despairing Emperor shot himself with a pistol that had been presented to him by Queen Victoria in the happier years of his reign.

Theodore's death left the field open to the rebellious forces that had been seething throughout his rule. By 1872, however, Ethiopia had a new King of Kings, the Emperor Yohannes IV, who had succeeded in dominating Tigré in the north. Shoa, in the central part of the country, was under the control of Prince Menelik, who had managed to escape from Magdala even before the death of Theodore.

To add to Ethiopia's problems at the time, the Suez Canal had been opened in 1869, paving the way for Egyptian and European entry into the Red Sea directly from the Mediterranean. Ethiopia's Red Sea coast and the remaining coastal area of the horn of Africa were now easily accessible to whatever naval powers chose to approach them. By 1875, the Egyptians had managed to slip through the Suez Canal and launch attacks on the Ethiopian coast. While Yohannes IV battled them, Menelik continued to consolidate his Shoan domain bringing into it the Galla south and west.

The opening of the Suez Canal brought another foreign threat to Ethiopia's security. Starting in 1869, when a local sultan had sold the Red Sea port town of Assab to Florio-Rubattine, an Italian trading and navigation company, Italy had been making inroads in Ethiopia. In 1885, after some Italian missionaries had been murdered by coastal Ethiopian tribesmen, the Italian government took over the port of Assab and occupied Massawa as well, both in Eritrea.

During the period that followed, Emperor Yohannes IV was occupied with putting down a fanatical Moslem sect from the Sudan that was ravaging the western borderlands of Ethiopia. In 1889, Yohannes IV was killed in battle against the Moslems, leaving Menelik of Shoa the strongest ruler in Ethiopia.

* * *

Addis Ababa, with Mount Entoto in the distance

Menelik was crowned Emperor of Ethiopia in 1889. His capital, located in the very heart of the central province of Shoa, was called Addis Ababa (New Flower) and was the most southerly of all the imperial capitals the Empire had known.

One of Menelik's first acts was the signing of the Treaty of Ucciale with Italy in May, 1889. By this treaty, Menelik officially granted the Italians the stronghold they had established in Eritrea. In return he received financial aid and European arms with which to expand and protect the borders of the southern half of Ethiopia. The Italian presence in Eritrea also relieved Menelik of the burden of maintaining control of the coastal tribes and the rebellious Tigrean elements in the north.

The terms of the treaty soon revealed that a misunder-

The hilltop mausoleum of Emperor Menelik II in Addis Ababa

standing had taken place, however, and relations between Menelik and the Italians began to be strained. In the Italian version, the treaty stated that the Emperor of Ethiopia *consented* to consult the Italian government in all his dealings with foreign powers. In the Amharic version, which Menelik insisted was the correct one, the treaty stated that the Emperor *might*, if he so desired, consult the Italian government in such matters.

The real question was how much control Italy actually had over Ethiopia. This issue came to the test in November, 1895, when a military struggle broke out between the two nations.

On March 2, 1896, an Italian force that had invaded Tigré, in Ethiopia proper, was defeated on the plain of Adowa by the well-equipped army of Menelik II. The Italians were permitted to keep their colony of Eritrea, but the unqualified independence of the Empire of Ethiopia was established through Menelik's victory. The anniversary of the Italian defeat at Adowa is celebrated on March 2 and is known as Adowa Day.

Menelik died in 1913, having accomplished the first difficult steps toward bringing Ethiopia into the modern age. Although he left the Italians in control of Eritrea, he otherwise unified and expanded the Empire and fixed the borders of Ethiopia very much as they are today.

He established relations with foreign governments, helped Ethiopia to acquire its first railroad, which connected the new capital of Addis Ababa with the sea, established the country's first banking institution, established a postal service, and had electricity, telephone, and telegraph systems installed. He opened the first public school, gave permission for Western missionary schools in Ethiopia, and sent the first young Ethiopians abroad to study. In the area of public health, he spurred the first vaccination campaigns for Ethiopia. He was almost certainly the greatest emperor Ethiopia had yet known.

In failing health in the last years of his life, Menelik II designated his young relative, Lij Yasu, as his successor. Lij Yasu proved unsatisfactory. The young man had strong leanings toward Islam and himself became a convert to the religion of Mohammed, an act which cost him the powerful and all-important support of the Ethiopian Christian Church. In 1916, Lij Yasu was deposed and Menelik's daughter, Zauditu, became Empress.

Ras Tafari Makonnen, son of the governor of Hararge Province, was chosen to serve as regent with his cousin, Empress Zauditu. By 1928, he was declared *negus* (king) and in

1930, upon the death of Zauditu, he ascended the throne as His Imperial Majesty Haile Selassie I, King of Kings, Elect of God, Conquering Lion of the Tribe of Judah. "Haile Selassie," the throne name that Ras Tafari chose as emperor, means "power of the Trinity."

The Emperor was born near the city of Harar on July 23, 1892. As regent, he represented the progressive element in a conservative, lackluster government. Even in the 1920's he was ably conducting foreign affairs for Ethiopia and had secured his country's admission to the League of Nations. Upon becoming *negus* in 1928, Ras Tafari negotiated a twenty-year Treaty of Friendship with Italy, calling for a free-trade zone at the port of Assab and the construction of roads to the interior.

In 1931, a year after ascending the throne, the new Emperor gave Ethiopia its first constitution. This document was revised and liberalized in 1955. At present, Ethiopia's constitution provides for a parliament consisting of a Senate, with its members appointed by the emperor, and a Chamber of Deputies, with its members elected by the people. There is also a cabinet called the Council of Ministers, appointed by the emperor. The right to vote is granted to all Ethiopian men and women who are citizens by birth and have reached the required age.

The government of Ethiopia is defined as a constitutional monarchy. However, full sovereignty and supreme authority still rest with the emperor. The constitution provides for succession to the throne by the oldest son of the emperor—in the case of Emperor Haile Selassie, Crown Prince Asfa Wossen.

Like the monarchs who preceded him, one of Haile Selassie's first tasks, and a continuing one, was that of placing responsible and loyal men around the country as provincial governors and other local officials. Throughout the long years of his reign, the Emperor exhibited a genius for balancing the claims and counterclaims of the many factions around him and for utilizing foreign advisors, especially in the training of security forces and in matters of administrative organization. Above all he steadfastly maintained his position as a father figure to his people, personally directing the affairs of the Empire during its period of greatest change.

During the 1920's and 1930's, under the Fascist dictatorship of Benito Mussolini, Italy still remembered with resentment the defeat of the Italian forces at Adowa in 1896. Compared with other European nations in the 1930's, Italy had meager colonial possessions in Africa—only Eritrea on the northern fringe of Ethiopia and Italian Somaliland on Ethiopia's southeastern border. However, these two possessions were strategically placed, like a pair of pincers embracing the large nugget that was Ethiopia itself. By 1934, Mussolini was informing the Italian people that it was their "duty" to bring a "civilizing" influence to the horn of Africa.

The incident that sparked the Italo-Ethiopian War of 1935 and 1936 took place in the Ogaden, the dry scrubby wasteland of southeastern Ethiopia, with its scarce and precious water holes. At a place called Walwal, about sixty miles inside the Ethiopian border, Somali nomads of Ethiopia, as well as those of Italian Somaliland, were in the habit of gathering to water their herds.

Some years earlier Italian troops based in Italian Somaliland had crossed the fuzzily defined border into Ethiopia and built fortifications at Walwal. In December, 1934, a skirmish developed there between Italian and Ethiopian troops. The Fascist government of Italy demanded an apology and financial compensation from the Ethiopian government. Ethiopia's refusal gave Italy the excuse it was seeking to take further military action.

The League of Nations failed to act against these early demonstrations of Italian aggression against Ethiopia, and in 1935 Italy launched a full-scale invasion of Ethiopia.

His Imperial Majesty Haile Selassie I
crowned Emperor of Ethiopia in 1930

In a cruel and one-sided military contest, the Italian command used aerial bombing, machine guns, heavy artillery, and poison gas against Ethiopian warriors, most of whom were barefoot, clad in lion skins, and armed with spears. Ethiopia, totally defenseless, was used as a testing ground for the air assaults that were to follow in World War II. Less sophisticated weapons were also employed. In some instances, the Fascists spread the ground with broken glass to block the escape routes of barefoot Ethiopian soldiers who were being attacked with mustard gas.

In seven months' time the Ethiopians had been decisively beaten. On May 2, 1936, the Emperor and members of the royal family fled Addis Ababa by means of the railway to Djibouti. Their escape took place only hours before the Italian troops, moving rapidly down from the north, cut the line to prevent further departures. Three days later, on May 5, Italian occupation troops entered Addis Ababa. Ethiopia was now incorporated, along with Eritrea and Italian Somaliland into an Italian colonial possession known as Italian East Africa.

The Emperor arrived in London in June, 1936. On June 30 he spoke before the League of Nations. In a proud but touching speech he challenged the world body regarding "the value of promises made to small states" concerning their integrity and independence. With immense dignity, the five-foot two-inch monarch told the League, "God and history will remember your judgment." The Emperor remained in exile in England during most of the five-year Italian occupation of Ethiopia.

In 1939, World War II broke out in Europe. Italy's declaration of war against the Allies in June, 1940, brought Great Britain into direct conflict with Italy in East Africa.

The British-led war to drive the Italians out of Ethiopia was relatively swift, requiring only about six months of fighting.

On May 5, 1941, exactly five years from the day Italian troops had entered Addis Ababa, the Emperor returned to the capital and to his throne. In his "mercy proclamation" to his people, Haile Selassie asked that they refrain from committing acts of vengeance against the departing Italians despite the barbarous and savage treatment inflicted on Ethiopians. The Emperor begged his people not to "spoil the good name of Ethiopia by acts which are worthy of the enemy."

May 5, the anniversary of the Emperor's return, is celebrated as Liberation Day in Ethiopia. It is an occasion for pride and rejoicing but also for deep sadness.

The years following the 1941 liberation saw a marked leap forward on the domestic front, while in external affairs Ethiopia plunged into the mainstream of world events.

Since much of the past had been destroyed and many of the old traditions had been weakened by the war and the occupation, the Emperor was able to start afresh in many areas such as education, health and welfare, national security, and civil and criminal law. He was also able to bring about certain reforms. Slavery, which had plagued Ethiopia from earliest times, was abolished. And, acknowledging Ethiopia's large Moslem population, the Emperor wrote complete freedom of religion into the 1955 constitution.

Eritrea, which had been administered by Great Britain after 1941, was loosely federated with Ethiopia in 1952. In 1962, Eritrea became part of the Empire, as one of its fourteen provinces. This provided Ethiopia with much-needed access to the sea through the ports of Massawa and Assab.

The 1955 constitution was an attempt, on the Emperor's

part, to modernize and liberalize the Ethiopian system of government. In making the Chamber of Deputies a popularly elected body instead of an appointed one, as it had been previously, it opened the way for representative government. But many of the young, educated Ethiopians with progressive ideas were dissatisfied. They felt that this and other provisions of the new constitution were meaningless. There were still no political parties in Ethiopia, the Emperor still had the right to veto all legislation, and the system still concentrated supreme power in the hands of the Emperor.

The Emperor might have been showing liberal tendencies that were shocking to the traditionalists in Ethiopia. But for the reform element, observing the popular uprisings in other African countries against their colonial masters, the Emperor was proceeding toward democratization much too slowly, if indeed at all.

These discontents finally came to a head with an attempted coup against the Emperor in 1960. It took place on December 13 and 14, while His Majesty was on a state visit to Brazil. The reform leaders included the commander of the Imperial Bodyguard and several other high-ranking officers. Initially the organized forces supporting the coup appeared to be successful, but they were soon opposed and easily defeated by army units loyal to the Emperor. Order was restored even before the Emperor returned to Addis Ababa.

Blood had been shed on both sides. The leaders of the coup assassinated the cabinet ministers and the other loyal government leaders whom they had taken hostage. The rebel leaders were either killed in the fighting or later tried and executed. The coup had had the support of most of the Addis Ababa university students. However, the Emperor extended a mass pardon to them after they had apologized.

Addis Ababa's Africa Hall, home of
the Organization of African Unity

Although some observers predicted there would be repeated unrest, sparked by Ethiopian reform elements influenced by Western liberal social and political ideas, the decade following the 1960 coup was quiet. In part, this was due to the Emperor's wisdom in granting some additional reforms after the attempted coup. At the same time, the Emperor embarked on a policy to bring his country into leadership among the emerging nations of independent Africa, setting Ethiopia up as a center for pan-Africanism.

In 1963, the Emperor sponsored a Conference of African Chiefs of State at Addis Ababa. The meeting resulted in the Organization of African Unity, which today numbers over forty African member nations. The OAU seeks full cooperation and political unity for the independent countries of Africa and is dedicated to the elimination of colonialism on the African continent.

In making Addis Ababa the home of the Permanent Secretariat of the OAU, Haile Selassie made it the hub for African affairs. The OAU meets in Africa Hall, an impressive modern structure facing on a broad avenue directly across from the Emperor's Jubilee Palace. Africa Hall today houses both the Organization of African Unity and the United Nations Economic Commission for Africa.

During January and February, 1972, Ethiopia, a charter member of the United Nations, played host to a week-long

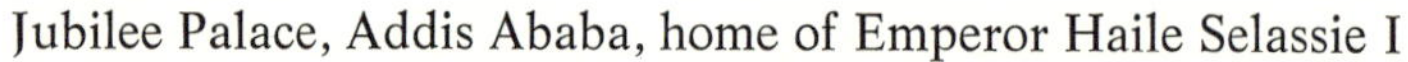

Jubilee Palace, Addis Ababa, home of Emperor Haile Selassie I

special session of the Security Council at Africa Hall. The Council met away from its New York City headquarters for the first time in twenty years, in order to discuss African affairs on African soil.

Today Emperor Haile Selassie I is the longest-reigning monarch of his time and is warmly regarded throughout the world as an elder statesman of considerable prestige and dignity. He is still making state visits abroad, as has been his lifelong custom.

In matters of foreign policy, Ethiopia pursues a course of nonalignment. It opposed the United States military involvement in Vietnam as it did the Soviet Union's invasion of Czechoslovakia.

Relations with most foreign countries are good, but there are continuing trouble spots on Ethiopia's borders with Somalia and the Sudan, owing to border claims and to Moslem-Christian conflicts. This situation is aggravated by the activities of the Eritrean Liberation Front, an Arab-dominated organization that advocates the separation of Eritrea from Ethiopia because of Eritrea's large Moslem population. Ethiopia charges that the Sudan and countries of the Arab world, particularly Syria, actively support the ELF. Incidents of violence have been reported from time to time in Eritrea due to the guerrilla activities of the ELF and the retaliatory actions of the Ethiopian security forces stationed there.

At the same time, Ethiopia has been strengthening ties with Israel. Both peoples claim descent from King Solomon and so share a similar heritage. Both countries, one Christian, one Jewish, find themselves surrounded by Moslem peoples.

On the Ethiopian domestic scene, the major question for the future is whether the reform elements of the Ethiopian people will demand self-rule from their leaders, as the peoples of other African countries have from their colonial masters, or whether, in a country with a tradition of government by its own religious and ethnic rulers, there will be a willingness to work in a gradual, orderly fashion toward democratization.

As long as the Emperor retains command, it is unlikely that major changes will come about on either the domestic or foreign fronts. However, the question for the near future, the question of what happens in Ethiopia "after the Emperor," remains open.

Just as Emperor Haile Selassie has managed to serve as a mediating factor for the jarring elements in his own country, he has helped to bridge the differences among nations of the world and particularly among African nations. Surely the most significant achievement for Haile Selassie I and for Ethiopia in the present era has been the emergence of the "land of the lion," Africa's oldest independent state, as a center for summit-level discussion of African problems and as a leader among the continent's newly independent nations.

GLOSSARY

abuna: principal official, holding rank of patriarch, in the Ethiopian Monophysite Church
amba: flat-topped hill, common in the highlands
ato: Mr.
azmari: minstrellike folk singers
berberi: powdered spice prepared from very sharp dried red peppers
chat (also *khat*)*:* a green shrub whose leaves have narcotic properties and are chewed as a stimulant
dabo kolo: small bits of baked flour dough eaten as a snack
dabtara: a cantor, scribe, religious scholar, with no ecclesiastical status
dega: cool highland zone with elevations of 8000 or more feet
demera: tepeelike arrangement of tall wooden poles decorated with daisies, part of Maskal celebration
doro wat: a hot chicken stew with hard-cooked eggs in it
dula: long wooden staff carried by foot travelers
Enkutatash: Ethiopian New Year's Day
Fasika: Ethiopian Easter
fukara: folk song telling of a warrior's bravery
gebeta: a game like chess
Genna: Ethiopian Christmas; also *genna,* a game similar to hockey played on Christmas Day
guks (or *yeferas guks*)*:* exhibition game of brilliant horsemanship performed at Timkat, Maskal, and special state occasions
gursha: an offering of *injera* and *wat* which the host places directly into a guest's mouth as a hospitality gesture

ichegé: the head of Ethiopia's principal monastery, the spiritual leader of all Ethiopian monks

injera: thin, flexible, spongy, pancakelike bread

kabaro: oblong, tapering drum with skin stretched over both ends

k'amis: white cotton dress with full skirt

kes: priest of the Ethiopian Monophysite Church

kolo: grain, usually refers to a mixture of roasted whole kernels of various cereal grains

krar: lyrelike musical instrument, usually with six strings

kwolla: low-lying hot-climate zone

lalibeloch: traditional folk singers who serenade incognito

leqso: folk song telling of misfortunes or general unhappiness

makamiya: Ethiopian priest's prayer stick

masinko: single-stringed musical instrument with a diamond-shaped wooden box, played with a bow

Maskal: religious holiday marking the finding of the True Cross

Maskarem: first month of Ethiopian year

masob: table of woven straw used for serving meals

megallah: marketplace

metad: large earthenware or iron disc used for baking *injera*

mousho: folk song composed for funerals

negus: king

Pagumen: last month of Ethiopian year

qené: an ancient form of Ethiopian verse

ras: a noble, usually the equivalent of a prince or duke

salgo: a Lenten dish of ground dried peas and beans stewed with spices

shamma: three-yard-long white cotton shawl worn like a toga over upper part of body by Amhara and Tigrean men and women

shilela: patriotic folk song

tabot: carved rectangular tablet of wood or stone representing the Ark of the Covenant

talla: home-brewed beer made from barley

tanqua: slim, curved boat made of bundles of papyrus reeds

teff: millet flour

tej: national alcoholic drink made from fermented honey

Timkat: Epiphany, a major religious holiday

tsenatsel: a rattlelike percussion instrument used in religious dances and processions

tukul: round native hut with mud-plaster walls and a cone-shaped thatched roof

washint: simple bamboo flute with four finger holes
wat: a spicy stew, with or without meat
woina dega: "highland of the grape"; temperate climate zone with elevations of 5000 to 8000 feet
woizerit: Miss
woizero: Mrs., lady
zaffran: folk song about simple everyday emotions or events
zar: evil spirit
zegeni: Tigrinya for *wat*

BIBLIOGRAPHY

Barker, A. J., *The Civilizing Mission: A History of the Italo-Ethiopian War*. New York, Dial, 1968

Busk, Douglas, *The Fountain of the Sun: Unfinished Journeys in Ethiopia and the Ruwenzori*. London, Max Parrish, 1957

Buxton, David, *The Abyssinians*. New York and Washington, Praeger, 1970

Buxton, David, *Travels in Ethiopia*. New York and Washington, Praeger, 1967

Coughlan, Robert, and *Life* Editors, *Tropical Africa*. New York, Time-Life Books, 1970

Jäger, Otto A., *Antiquities of Northern Ethiopia: A Guide*. Stuttgart, Brockhaus, 1965

Kaplan, Irving, and others, *Area Handbook for Ethiopia*. Washington, U.S. Government Printing Office, 1971

Levine, Donald N., *Wax and Gold: Tradition and Innovation in Ethiopian Culture*. Chicago, University of Chicago Press, 1965

Moorehead, Alan, *The Blue Nile*. New York, Harper & Row, 1962

Ullendorff, Edward, *The Ethiopians: An Introduction to Country and People*. London, Oxford University Press, 1965

INDEX

* indicates illustrations

INDEX